ARIEL

ARIEL

BY

JOSÉ ENRIQUE RODÓ

TRANSLATED, WITH AN INTRODUCTORY ESSAY

BY

F. J. STIMSON (J. S. OF DALE)
Late United States Ambassador to Argentina

BOSTON AND NEW YORK

HOUGHTON MIFFLIN COMPANY

The Riverside Press Cambridge

JOSÉ ENRIQUE RODÓ

Prefatory Essay

ONE day last year, some three years after his death at Palermo alone and in distress, a Uruguayan ship of war brought home, to his native city of Montevideo, Rodo's body — to be buried beneath the great monument his nation is now to dedicate to him. The day was made a national holiday, and all Latin America, in sympathy, took part.

Although perhaps the greatest of modern American idealists, and the London *Times*, the Boston *Transcript*, the New York *Prensa*, devoted pages to his memory, he is still little known in North America. "ARIEL," perhaps his greatest work, has much to say of us; it is charged with a spirit that in these post-war days we have largely lost; it brings the best thought of that older, Latin, Roman culture of Amer-

ica of the South to the newer, Saxon civilization of the North; it has been therefore
a grateful task for a representative of the
latter to essay its translation, with a hope
of saving something of the beauty of the
original. For "ARIEL" is a thing of *beauty*,
first of all; its learning, if not its teaching,
might be gleaned from other books.

South America believes, with many of
us, that in the ideals of America rest the
hope of the world. And in this all-Amer-
ican mission, South America has its share.
The Saxon gift to the world's civilization
was liberty; the Roman, was law; the one
excels in applied science, the other in the
Art of Life; and both, in America, are
dreaming of a world where there is no
war. But South America, in an age of
brute conflict, a time of chemistry and of
machines, when the flood of materialism
seemed about to overcome the finer work
of civilization, has, by its very remoteness,
its very backwardness, been held aloof.

Although with a passionate interest greater then than ours, it viewed the war for the most part as a distant planet a burning sun. And before that cataclysm, to which the world's machine-made industrialism indeed had largely led, its countries, mainly agricultural, were spared that flood of energy for the multiplication of the cheaper things of life, not food for body or the soul, that slavery to machines in the much-vaunted "efficiency," and "division of labor," that exploitation of man and woman in the operative, which have so much confused our Northern judgment of the higher things in life, and, worse than that, has bred class-conflict, distrust of all government, and passionate enmity between those who should be working together in generous production and fair distribution of even the material things of earth.

John Stuart Mill had a horrible phrase : " *Utilities, fixed and embodied in material objects* " ; and it has lately seemed, in that world of chemistry and machinery which our modern life has evolved, as if only those utilities which could be fixed and embodied in material objects and multiplied in great quantities for universal demand were deemed of any value. Newspapers instead of books, "process" work for pictures, "movies" for plays, casts for sculpture, moulds of concrete for architecture, and, worst of all, canned food or cold-storage for fresh vegetables, meat, or fish, and ready-bought "delicatessen" replacing the art of cooking; commercial textbooks and state-schedules for the individual teacher; trusts for the private initiative; and everywhere, machinery for handicraft, "applied science" for the arts, and crowd-imitation or the mob-spirit for the free mind. But Ruskin followed Mill; and he asked humanity to consider what "value" really means. It is not material, still less mechanical, but the *life-giving* quality of a thing: *valor — valere —* that which is sane, and well, and makes for the life of man; and that means, in last analysis, the life of his soul. Moving men, or their merchandise, or even their messages, at lightning speed from place to place, does not better humanity nor much improve man's civilization; nor does the multiplication of brute objects without beauty or value in themselves. *Value* may be defined as that which gives strength to life and elevation to the soul. Beauty does this; and purity of thought; and high knowledge, both of past and present; and these are works of art and of teaching, not of science. And virtue, which is the word *value* as applied to the spirit, is born of thought and bred to character. And the great thoughts of men are saved for other men mainly by books. Thus we find that it is art and literature which are true value to the soul, as right acting and true thinking make the character of man. Science should be the handmaiden of life, the

hewer of wood and the drawer of water;
the *Caliban*, in short. But the souls of
men will starve as the ideals of men will
fail, when they forget their *Ariel*.

We live in a time when Caliban seems
to have the upper hand. The desires of
Caliban, the judgments of Caliban, the
hunger and thirst of Caliban, seem now
to fill the world. And some of us are losing heart. We feel as if there were no
master Prospero, no mage to bind and
scourge Caliban back to his lair, to plague
him with the pains of his own shortcom-
ing, to punish his coarse body with cramps
and pains, the retribution, the Nemesis
that came in Shakespeare's *Tempest* to
subdue even Caliban once more to his spirit
master. The voices that see this and protest aloud are few. There were almost
none in Germany. The world of materialism was all that her misguided people saw.
Sometimes there did not seem to be many
in our own country, where the numbing

stream of sudden wealth had lured man's coarser nature to self-indulgence, and a luxury to which it was unused had stunted —let us hope, but for the moment—the growth of his soul.

Yet, living is an art, and not a science. "Conduct is three-fourths of life"; and conduct in itself is an art; the art of right living. And *value*—that is, what makes for the real welfare of humanity—depends upon the *wholesome* things alone, beginning with healthy food; for man's first art was the art of cooking; and ending in the art of making a beautiful house, a happy home, right teaching and right thinking for the children; and the enlargement of man's nature in the higher freedom of the soul.

It seems to be a time when the multitude is contemptuous of all this. Hod-carriers are paid more than teachers; while as for thinkers, artists, poets, the world now seems to have no use for them. For five years it has devoted itself to the manufacture of mechanisms to destroy human life; only a tithe of its effort has been devoted even to the raising of food, to the things that have value, that have the power of giving life, life of the body or life of the spirit. And yet men are puzzled! They complain of the high cost of living, when for a lustrum men have not thought of living but of killing; they marvel that those things of real value, which the world has neglected to plant or rear, have grown so scarce. And in North America we do not yet seem to have profited by this lesson. Caliban has there no word for Ariel, and all that Ariel represents. They call him scornfully the "highbrow"; that is to say, the man who has behind his forehead sight and thought for things that lie above and beyond immediate sensuous enjoyment. Sadly significant is the use of this scornful piece of slang — "highbrow" — for all that stands above what swine may trample with their feet.

Yet there have been voices, and voices since Ruskin, who have spoken in protest of all this. In Italy, Ferrero; in Uruguay, Rodó; Amado Nervo in Mexico; the poets of Colombia, and poets and publicists in Argentina. Why is it that so many of these come from South America, and all that I have mentioned are of Latin stock?

South Americans have sometimes thought themselves unfortunate that they were so far removed from the great material movements of the day; that they spring from an ancient Latin race, not of lusty Northern blood, and that for three centuries since they have kept mainly to themselves by preserving the Spanish traditions of manners and of life. They have valued personal dignity as they have valued courtesy; personal liberty as much as State power; less interested in machinery than in the art of life; they have placed "*la joie de vivre*" above the making wholesale of "utilities fixed and embodied in material objects.'' And possibly some of them have repined that they were weak countries, not strong materially, not bristling with navies or great armies. They have not seen — nor does the world yet see — what a rare rôle they have to play. Of all the quarters of the world, this alone has been able to keep tranquilly burning the torch of civilization. Here they have had no dream of conquest, and no harsh necessity of protecting themselves. The war has been remote, even in those South American countries which engaged in it; and before the war the very fact that they were not countries of great material prosperity other than that healthy well-being which comes direct from the soil; that they were not dazzled by all the temptations of exploiting the masses in hived industries — enabled them to keep Caliban in his place. It is not a trivial thing that of all countries of the world the Latin-American ones are those where poets are most numerous and all that poetry stands for is most prized. It is not without significance that South America alone is almost free, so far as Americans are concerned, from the "I Won't Worker" who would spoliate the labor of others and do without all but the grosser things of this world — and from the legislative meddler and from the Bolshevik. For the same reason, International Law, which is the shield of weak countries against the strong, has its natural home in South America; and many of its leading scholars live there. For if liberty be the great gift to the world of the Saxon civilizations, law is the lesson of the Latin. And bound together and protected by bonds of fraternity which shall forever guard them against foreign aggression, they have been able to keep this lamp burning undimmed. The spirit of Cervantes is still with them, as in that wonderful chapter wherein he talks on war. Long may it be before it is forgotten! The object of war is peace, as the object of life is joy; and joy cannot endure without the love of one's fellow-men.

This work of Rodó's, when it first appeared, some years since, lay in piles of popular editions in every bookstall in Buenos Aires and other South American cities. One can hardly hope for such a general reading here. But it is a typical message from South America; and, as such, well worth our attention. Spanish scholars will note that (in order to conform their way of writing to ours in English) I have a little simplified the style of Rodó, particularly toward the end. Barring this, I hope that it is faithfully reproduced; and that in the process of translating, not all the beauty of the marvellous Spanish has been lost.

What would Rodó have said, had he lived to see our entrance in the great war for world liberty? And how much would he have altered or added to what he says

of the United States in ARIEL? Much, by
very much. Indeed for several years before the war there had been noticeable a
marked change in the feelings of intelligent South Americans toward their
big brother, the erstwhile feared "Colos-
sus of the North." Although Manuel
Ugarte in South America, with Zimmer-
mann of the Berlin Foreign Office, tried
vainly to keep it alive in the interests of
Germany during the war, this distrust of
us had been rapidly disappearing. That
very spirit of ideality which Rodó in this
book finds so largely lacking had shown
itself powerful enough to lead us, with
motives at least immediately unselfish, into
the greatest war of history. For years before, ever since the Spanish War, in fact
(which in its inception they had bitterly
disapproved), our course, as shown in
Cuba, in the Philippines, and, despite all
our provocation, as to Mexico; in President Wilson's Mobile speech; in the treaty

making amends to Colombia; and finally
in the reasons given in his address to Con-
gress on declaring war—had met with
South American approval. They feared us
no longer. And when they read our reasons
then given for our entrance into the war,
what had been fear became enthusiasm.
In Argentina, where up to that time English and German influences, equally strong,
had about divided public sentiment, it became, from fifty-fifty "pro-aliado" quite
ninety per cent "pro-Americano." Argentina refused to issue a decree of neutrality
as between the United States and Germany,
although one had been issued, in 1914, as
between Germany and the other powers;
and a great mass meeting was held in the
largest theater in Buenos Aires to encour-
age the Government to extend open hospitality to Caperton's fleet during the war,
at which our action was compared to the
great heroic epic of South America when,
a hundred years before, their great liber-

ator, San Martín, had led an Argentine
army across the almost unknown Andes
to free Chile and Peru, and then, with the
help of Bolivar, all Spanish South America from the yoke of Spain. San Martín's
rifles had been sent him in a Boston ship:
and the ladies of Mendoza had sold their
jewels to buy the metals of which to cast
his cannon. And in the city of Mendoza
there is to-day, on a foothill of the Andes,
perhaps the greatest of modern monuments, to commemorate this event.

"You have," said one orator of the
occasion, referring first to their "Cabildo,"
in Buenos Aires, their "cradle of liberty,"
and then to their Independence Hall, the
old house in the city of Tucumán where
their independence was formally declared,
"a third great and solemn monument. It
stands on the Hill of Glory, and looks
Westward to the peaks of the Andes. It
bears thousands of figures in bronze and
others sculptured from the living rock;

and they commemorate the devotion and the abnegation of the Argentine people and the valour of their march across the Andes under San Martín's leadership. And now we judge your entrance into the great war for the freedom of Europe's peoples as that great épopée of San Martín guiding us Argentines across the snows of the Andes to liberate the peoples of America. North America is crossing the Atlantic now, as South America crossed the Andes then.''

So the Argentine people ; and the Argentine Government answered our note declaring the war on Germany with a note expressing sympathy with our reasons given and recognizing the justice of our cause.

And Uruguay?

Rodó did not live to see it ; but when our fleet came down, during the war, and there was question whether it should be permanently received or coldly restricted

to its twenty-four hours' stay permitted a
belligerent by international law in a neutral country, Uruguay, in a published
decree, refused to be neutral in a war
where America was fighting for liberty
and right. An original copy of this decree,
signed by the Uruguayan President and
Cabinet, was presented by him to the
translator. This is its translation:

MONTEVIDEO, 18 of June of 1917

Considering that in divers communications the
Government of Uruguay has proclaimed the
principle of American solidarity as controlling
its international politics, meaning thereby that
any aggression on the rights of one American
country should be considered such by all and
provoke in all a uniform and common reaction;
and that, in the hope that an accord to that effect
might be realized among the nations of America
which would make possible the practical and efficient realization of this ideal, this Government has
adopted an attitude of expectancy as to its action,
although expressing its sympathy in each case
with such American countries as have been
obliged to abandon their neutrality;

Considering that, even while such accord has not been realized, Uruguay cannot, without going against her sentiments and her convictions, treat like belligerents those American countries which in defence of their rights now find themselves engaged in an intercontinental war;

Considering that this judgment meets with the approval of the Honourable Senate;

The PRESIDENT of the REPUBLIC
in Council General of Ministers
Resolves:

FIRST. To declare that no American country which in defence of its rights finds itself in a state of war with nations of other continents shall be treated as a belligerent.

SECOND. To decree that no dispositions shall be made contrary to this resolution.

THIRD. Be this communicated and published, etc.

Such was the opinion of Rodó's country in 1917. It is hardly likely that that of Rodó would have been otherwise.

F. J. S.

,BUENOS AIRES, *April*, 1921

ARIEL

ARIEL

ON that evening the venerable old master whom we used to call Prospero, after the wise sage of Shakespeare's "Tempest," was bidding good-bye to his young scholars, met about him for the last time after a long year of task work.

They had come to the lofty hall of study, where a taste at once refined and austere sought to do honour to the noble presence of books, Prospero's faithful companions. But the leading note of the hall — like a divinity, serene in its nimbus — was a finely wrought bronze, representing Ariel in "The Tempest."

It was the manner of the Master to sit close by this bronze statue; and that was why he was called by the name of the magician who in the play is loved and served by the spirit of fancy that the sculptor had sought to embody.

But perhaps, as well in the manner of his teaching, or in his character, there were a reason for the nickname, in profounder sense. Ariel, genius of the Air, represents, in the symbolism of Shakespeare, the noble part — the spirit with wings. . . . For Ariel embodies the mastery of reason and of sentiment over the baser impulses of unreason. He is the generous zeal, the lofty and disinterested motive in action, the spirituality of civilization, and the vivacity and grace of the intelligence ; — the ideal end to which human selection aspires ; that superman in whom has disappeared, under the persistent chisel of life, the last stubborn trace of the *Caliban*, symbol of sensuality and stupidity.

The little statue, a real work of art, reproduced the Spirit of the Air at the moment where, freed by the magic of Prospero, he is about to soar into the sky, there to vanish in a lightning flash.

With spread-out wings, in a loose and floating garment which the caress of the light upon the bronze damascened into gold, his broad forehead lifted up, his lips just opening with a tranquil smile, all of Ariel's attitude most admirably showed that gracious moment just preceding flight; and, with happy inspiration, the same art which had given the image its sculptured limbs had succeeded in preserving in his face that look of the seraph and the lightness of the ideal.

Prospero passed his hand, thoughtfully, over the head of the little statue; then, gathering a group of young men about him, with a firm voice — the voice of the Master, which, to pass its ideas and grave them deeply in the minds of the disciples, can employ either the clear penetration of a ray of light or the sharp blow of a chisel on the marble, the stroke of the painter's brush on canvas or the touch of the wave upon the sands to be read in fossils by future generations of men — the Master, as his scholars waited with affectionate attention, began to speak :

Near this statue where you have seen me preside each day over our talks as friends — talks which I hope have succeeded in dispelling from the work of teaching any touch of austerity — I have once more to speak to you, that our parting hour may be like the seal stamped upon our agreement both in feeling and in ideas. So I invoke Ariel as my divinity, and I could wish to-day for my lecture the most gentle and persuasive force that ever it has had, for I think that to speak to youth of noble motives, of lofty ideas, whatever they are, is as a kind of sacred oratory. I also think that the spirit of youth is as a generous soil, where the seed of an opportune word may in a short time return the fruits of an immortal harvest. I earnestly wish to coöperate with you in a page of that programme

which, in preparing yourselves for the free
air of action, you have doubtless formed in
your inner thought for the end of your efforts, the object to which each personality
shall devote his life. For that intimate, personal programme—which rarely is formu-
lated or written out, but more usually stays
within the breast until it is revealed in outer
action — fails never in the spirit of those
peoples or those persons who are something
above the rabble. If, with relation to individual liberty, Goethe could say so profoundly that only he is worthy of liberty and
life who can conquer it for himself each day;
with much more reason might I say that
the honour of every human generation requires that it shall conquer for itself, by
the persevering activity of its own thinking,
by the effort of its own will, its faith in the
determined, the persistent manifestation of
the ideal, and the place of the ideal in the
evolution of all ideas. And in conquering
your own you should begin by recogniz-

ing as the first object of faith your own selves. The youth which you love is a power whose application you must work yourselves, and a treasury for the use of which yourselves are responsible. Prize that treasure and that power ; see that the lofty consciousness of its possession stay radiant and effective in yourselves. I say to you with Renan : " Youth is the discovery of that immense horizon which is life." And the discovery which reveals unknown lands must be made complete with the virile force which shall rule them. No spectacle can be imagined more fit to captivate at once the interest of the thinker and the enthusiasm of the artist, than that which a human generation presents when it goes to meet a future all vibrant with the impatience of action, of lofty front, with a smiling and high disdain for deceit, the soul purified by sweet and distant mirages which wake in it mysterious impulses, like the visions of Cipango and

Eldorado in the heroical chronicles of the Conquistadores.

From the rebirth of human hopes; from the promises which ever trust to the future for the reality of a better thing, the soul acquires that beauty which opens at the breath of life; soft and unspeakable beauty, made up, as the dawn was for the poet of the "Contemplations," of "the trace of a dream, and the beginning of a thought."

Humanity, renewing from generation to generation its active hope and its anxious belief in an ideal, across the hard experience of centuries, made Guyau think of the obsession of that poor mad woman whose strange and touching madness consisted in thinking every day arrived the day of her marriage. The toy of her dream, every morning she bound to her pale forehead the nuptial crown and hung from her head the nuptial veil. With a sweet smile she then prepared to receive an imaginary bridegroom, all through the day to the shadows of the night, which put an end to the vain hope, and brought again disillusion to the heart. Then first her madness took a tint of melancholy; but her ingenuous trust reappeared with each aurora, and with no memory of the disenchantment of the evening, murmuring, "It's to-day that he comes," she turned again to bind herself with the nuptial veil and crown, smiling once more with the hope of the promised one.

It is thus, not as with the loss of an ideal that has died, that humanity clothes itself each era with its nuptial dress and expects with renewed faith the realization of the dreamed ideal — a persistent but touching folly. And to provoke this renewal, unalterable as the rhythm of nature, has been in all times the function and the work of youth. Of the souls of each human springtime is woven that bridal dress for mankind; and when one tries to suppress that sublime stubbornness of hope which is born all winged from the very breast of delusion, all pessimisms are in vain, as well those which are based on reason as those which come from experience. They have to confess themselves powerless to contravene that lofty *quand même* which springs from the depth of human life. There are times in which, by an apparent alteration of the triumphal rhythm, human history crosses generations destined to personify from the very cradle vacillation and disillusion. But these times pass — not perhaps without having had their own ideal like the others, though in negative form and of unconscious love — and again is lit up in the spirit of mankind the hope of the long-desired bridegroom; him whose image, sweet and radiant as in the ivory verses of the mystics, suffices to maintain the interest and content of life, although never to be incarnated in reality.

Youth, which thus signifies, in the soul of individuals and of generations, light, love, energy, exists and with the same meaning in the evolutionary processes of societies. Among these peoples who feel and look on life as you do, fecundity and force will always be the dominion of the future. Now there was an age when the attributes of man's youth made themselves more than in any other age the attributes of the whole people, the marks of an entire civilization, and in which a breath of youth's enchantment passed softly and touched the serene front of a whole race. When Greece was born, the gods awarded her the secret of youth inextinguishable; Greece is the soul when young. "He who in Delphi contemplates the pointed masses of the pines"—says one of the Homeric hymns—"imagines to himself that they must never grow old." Greece did mighty things because it had of youth the gaiety which is the atmosphere of action, and the enthusiasm which is the omnipotent lever. The Egyptian priest with whom

Solon spoke in the temple of Sais, said to the Athenian legislator, pitying the Greeks for their exuberant volubility: "You are only children." And Michelet has compared the activity of the Greek soul to a happy game, about which are grouped smiling all other nations on the earth. But of that divine game of children on the beaches of the Archipelago and in the shadow of the olives of Ionia, were born art, and philosophy, and free thought, and the curiosity of all investigation, and the consciousness of human dignity—all those God-given spurs which are yet our only inspiration and our pride. Absorbed in its hieratic austerity the country of the Egyptian priest represented only old age, old age given but to introspection, as if to practise for the repose of eternity, and waving aside any frivolous dream as with disdainful finger. Grace, inquietude, are proscribed from the attitudes of its soul, as was all action from its images of life. And when posterity turns its gaze upon Egypt, it meets only the sterile notion of order regulating the growth of a civilization which lived but to weave itself a shroud and build its tombs; the shadow of a sundial reaching out far over the sands of the desert.

The gifts of the youthful spirit — enthusiasm and hope — correspond in the harmonies of history and natural history to movement and to light. Wherever you shall turn your eyes you will find these, the natural atmosphere in which move all things that are strong and beautiful. Lift your eyes to the example most lofty of all, the idea of Christianity, over which even has weighed some accusation of having saddened the earth by proscribing the gaiety of paganism. Christianity itself is essentially an inspiration of youth, or was before it wandered from its cradle. New-born Christianity was in the interpretation of Renan — which I hold only the more true that it is the more poetic — a picture of

youth unsullied. Of the youth of the soul,
or, as is the same thing, of a living dream
of grace and purity, is made that divine
fragrance which floats over the slow jour-
neyings of the Master across the fields of
Galilee; over his sermons, which are developed, free of any penitent sadness, near
by a lovely lake, in valleys full of fruit;
heard by the birds of heaven and the "lilies
of the field," which thus adorn his par-
ables; preaching the happiness of the
"Kingdom of God" to a sweetly smiling
nature. From that happy picture are far
absent the ascetics who accompanied in
his solitude the penitences of John the
Baptist. When Jesus speaks of those who
follow him, he compares them to the
guests and bridesmaids of a wedding.
And that is the impression, one still of
divine contentment, which, embodied in
the essence of the new faith, one feels persist through all the Odyssey of the evan-
gelists; which sheds a radiant joy about

the spirit of the first Christian communities, an ingenuous joy of living, and which, going to Rome, opened easy passage to the hearts of the ignorant proselytes of the Transtevere. It triumphed by opposing the enchantment of the youth within them — embalsamed, as it were, by the libation of a new wine — to the severity of the Stoics and the decrepitude of the people of the Roman world.

Therefore, be ye conscious possessors of the blessed power you contain within yourselves. But do you never forget that this power is no more exempt than other virtuous impulses from weakening and disappearing if it be not carried into action. The gift of the precious treasure is from Nature; but on your own ideas depend whether it be fruitful or be vainly wasted, so scattered and dispersed among individual consciousnesses as never to appear a beneficent force on the life of human societies in general.

A profound critic has recently called attention in the pages of a novel—that immense surface mirror which seems to reflect the only image of our life these last hundred dizzy years—to the difference that exists between the soul of youth as portrayed in the time of "René" of Chateaubriand and the modern French novel. His analysis found a progressive diminution of "internal youth" and energy, between the heroes of romanticism and the enervated in heart and will, as shown in "A Rebours," or "Le Disciple." Yet a slight renascence of animation he hopefully noted in some more recent novels still, as in those of Lemaître, Wizewa, Rod, or even in "David Grieve," which shows in the title character all the troubles and unquiet ideals of several generations, only to resolve them at last in the supreme disentanglement of a happy love.

Shall this hope in truth be fulfilled? You, who like workmen to the factory are about to pass under the portals of the twentieth century—shall you shed over the arts you study images brighter and more glorious than were left by us who are about to leave you? If that divine age when youthful minds gave model to the dialogues of Plato were only possible in the short springtime of the world; if it is the rule "not to think on the Gods," as Forquias instructs the choir of captives in the second part of "Faust"—may we not at least dream of the coming of a human generation which shall return to life a sense of the ideal; a grand enthusiasm, when feeling may become a power, and when a vigorous rebirth of will-energy may expel from the bottom of our souls with shouts of victory those moral cowardices which are nurtured in our breasts by disappointment and by doubt? Shall again be youth the reality of our collective life, as it is that of the individuals?

That is the question which troubles me

as I look upon you. Your first pages as I read them, your confessions in them of your private life so far, speak often of indecision, of astonishment, but never of enervation or of definite loss of will. I am sure that enthusiasm is still a living force with you. I know well that those notes of discouragement and pain which the absolute sincerity of your thought — a virtue even greater than hope itself — has caused to spring from the tortures of your meditation in your sad but inevitable meetings with Doubt, were not an indication of a permanent soul-condition; and did not signify in any case your want of confidence in the eternal virtue-force of life. But when the cry of anguish rose to your lips from the depths of your hearts, you did not suffocate it before utterance, like the austere and proudly silent Stoic in his punishment, but ended your cry with an invocation to that ideal which "*shall come*" — as with the note of a Messianic inspiration.

On the other hand, though I speak to you of hope and enthusiasm as high and fertile virtues, I would by no means cross that inviolable line which divides scepticism from belief, illusion from happiness. Nothing is farther from my thought than to confound with the natural gifts of youth, with its beautiful spontaneity of spirit, that indolent frivolity of thinking, which, as it is incapable of seeing more than a gambler's motive in any human action, buys love, or tries to, buys life's pleasures at the cost of ignorance of all those things that may give one pause before the mysterious front, the solemn face of all realities. That is not the noble meaning of youth individual, or of the youth of peoples. I have always thought vain the policy of those statesmen, who shape America's policies and guard her fate, to suppress, before they ever reach our shores, any sound or echo of human suffering from the older world or its literature—fearing lest, morbid or unhealthy, it put in peril our fragile optimism. No firm training of the intelligence can be based on simple-minded isolation or on voluntary ignorance. Every problem proposed to human thought by the spirit of Doubt, every sincere reproach which is fulminated against Nature or against God himself from the breast of disheartenment or sorrow, has a right to reach our consciousness and there be considered and faced. The strength of our heart must show itself in accepting the riddle of the Sphinx; not in evading its awesome question.

Nor should you forget that even in bitterness of thought, as in joy, there may ever be a starting-point for action, often a fertile suggestion. When grief unmans, when it seems so irresistible as to prompt the abdication of the power to will, the philosophy which breeds such thoughts is unworthy of youthful souls. Then may the poet denounce "the slack soldier who fights beneath the flag of Death." But when there rises from the heart of sorrow the manly wish for battle, for conquest or reconquest of that boon which is denied us, then it becomes a double spur to action, most potent impulse to life. So Helvetius thought the very loathing of one's own lot a high prerogative of man, if, instead of dulling our sensibility in a slothful submission, it awaken it and become a spur to action. In that sense it has been well said that there are pessimisms which are like inverted optimism: far from supposing the renouncement and condemnation of all being, they teach, with their discontent of the actual, the necessity of its renewal. That which humanity needs, to be saved from all pessimistic negation, is not so much a belief that all is well at present, as the faith that it is possible through life's growth to arrive at a better state, hastened and discovered by the actions of men. Such faith in the future, belief in the efficacy of human energy, are the necessary condition of all strong action and all fecund thought. That is why I have wanted to begin with praising the eternal value of that faith which, being in youth a very instinct, needs the teaching of no dogma. For you all feel it stirring at the depths of your being, and know it for the divine suggestion of Nature itself.

Animated by this sentiment, enter you on life, its deep horizons before you, with the noble ambition of making your presence felt therein from the moment when you confront it with the glance of a conquistador. Join to the spirit of youth the initiative of the bold, the innovation of the genius. Perhaps everywhere to-day the action and the influence of youth is less effective in the march of human society than it ought to be, and less intense. Gaston Deschamps has noted it, in France, commenting on the tardy initiative of the younger generation in public life or culture, and the scanty original thought which they contribute to the beaten track of the prevailing ideas. My impressions of the present America, so far as I can form a general opinion, despite the sad isolation in which live its peoples, would perhaps justify a like remark. And yet I seem to see everywhere expressed a need for some active revelation of new forces; and I hold that America stands much in need of her youth. Here is the reason for which I speak to you. This is why I am so extraordinarily concerned with the moral development of your minds. The force of your word and your example may come to embody the living energies of the past in the work of the future. I hold with Michelet that the right idea of education does not include only the teaching to the minds of the sons the experience of the fathers, but as well, and often more, the informing of the fathers' experience with the innovating inspiration of the sons.

Let us then discuss how you shall consider the life that is awaiting you.

The divergence of individual vocations will impress divers directions upon your activities and cause to predominate in each one of you a disposition of mind predetermined by a definite aptitude. Some will be men of science, others of art, others still, of action. But over all the inclinations which may bind you severally to different tasks and ways of life, you should guard in your inner soul the consciousness of the fundamental unity of our nature, which demands that every human being be, above and before all, the unspoiled pattern of a man in whom no noble faculty of the mind be obliterated, and no lofty interest for all men have lost its communicative virtue. Before all modifications of profession and training stands the fulfilment of the destiny common to all rational beings. "There is one universal profession: — to be a man," says

Guyau. And Renan, remembering *à propos* of unbalanced and imperfect civilizations, that the end of the human creature cannot be only either to know or to feel or to imagine, but to be entirely and really human, defines the ideal of perfection to which he should bend his energies, as the possibility of offering in the individual type an abbreviated picture of the whole race.

Try, then, to develop so far as possible not any single aspect, but the plenitude of your being. Shrug not your shoulders before any noble and fecund manifestation of human nature, under the pretext that your own individuality ties you of preference to a different one. Be attentive spectators where you may not be actors. When that false and vulgarized idea of education, which thinks it subordinate wholly to utilitarian ends, takes upon itself to mutilate by such materialism the natural fulness of our minds, and by a premature specialization to proscribe the teaching of

anything that is disinterested or ideal,
it fails to avoid the danger of training
for the future minds that have become
narrow, incapable of seeing more than
the one aspect of a thing which immediately touches them, separated as by a
frozen desert from other minds that in the
same society have chosen other aspects of
our life. The necessity of devoting ourselves
each one to some determined activity, some
special form of learning, surely need not
exclude the inclination to realize, for the
intimate harmony of our spirit, that destiny which is common to all rational beings. That special activity must be but
the basic note of that harmony. The famous line in which the slave of the old
play affirmed that nothing human was
strange to him, being human himself,
forms part of that cry of the heart which
is eternal in the human consciousness because its meaning is inexhaustible. Our
capacity to understand must only be lim-

ited by the impossibility of understanding souls that are narrow. To be unable to see more than one phase of nature, more than one human interest or idea, is like living in the shadow of a dream pierced by a single ray of sunlight. That intolerance, that exclusiveness, which when born of tyrannous absorption in some high enthusiasm or flowing from some disinterested ideal may merit justification or even sympathy, becomes converted to the most abominable of inferiorities when in the circle of vulgar life it betrays the narrowness of a mind incapacitated to reflect on more than the partial appearances of things.

Unfortunately, in the very times when civilization reaches its highest level of culture is the danger of this limitation of minds most serious and its results most to be feared. For the law of evolution requires, as it appears in societies as well as individuals, an ever-increasing tendency to heterogeneity, which as the general cul-

ture of society increases limits individual
activities more and more and restricts the
field of action of each one to an ever-
narrower specialty. And though it be a
necessary condition of progress, this development of the notion of specialization
brings with it visible evils which not only
lower the horizon of the eye of thought,
thus distorting its image of the universe,
but come to injure also the spirit of human solidarity by the particularization of
individual habits and affections. Auguste
Comte well noted this peril of advanced
civilizations. A high state of social perfection had for him serious inconvenience
in that it facilitated the appearance of narrow and bounded minds; of brains "very
efficient under one aspect and monstrously
inept under all others." The belittling of
the human brain by continual exercise of
one mode of activity is compared by Comte
to the miserable lot of a labourer who by
the division of labour is condemned in a

factory to devote all the energies of his being to the invariable repetition of a single mechanical detail. In each case the moral result is to inspire him with a disastrous indifference to the general interests of humanity. And although this sort of human automatism does not, says the positivist, occur save under the extreme dispersive influence of the principle of specialization, its actual existence, already frequent, requires that we should give serious consideration to its importance.

This dispersive influence injures the beauty of our institutions no less than their strength. The incomparable beauty of Athens, the imperishable pattern left to humanity of all that is admirable and enchanting by her divine hand, lies in that that city of prodigies founded its idea of life on the concert of all human faculties, in the free and chartered liberty of all energies capable of contributing to the glory or the power of mankind! For Athens

alone could exalt at once the feeling for
ideal with the real, reason with instinct,
the forces of the body with those of the
spirit. It chiselled clear the four sides to
the soul. Every free Athenian draws, as it
were, a circle about him to contain his activities, a perfect circle in which no un-
ordered impulse shatters the graceful proportion of the line. He is athlete and living
sculpture in the gymnasium, citizen on
the Pnyx, polemic and thinker in the por-
ticoes. He exerts his will in every virile
action and his thought in any fertile task.
Therefore averred Macaulay that a day
in the public life of Athens comprised a
more brilliant programme of instruction
than any we now plan in our modern cen-
tres of education. And from that one free
blooming of the fulness of our nature rose
the miracle of Greece — an inimitable, enchanting mingling of animation and serenity, a springtime of the human spirit, a
smile of history.

In our times the growing complexity of our civilization would make unserious the thought of restoring this harmony, which is only possible with elements of a gracious simplicity. But within that very complexity of our culture, that progressive differentiation of our characters, our aptitudes, our merits, which is the unavoidable consequence of a progress in social evolution, it behooves us to preserve a reasonable share for all in certain basic ideas or feelings which alone keep up the unity and concert of human life — in certain *interests of the soul* for which the dignity of the rational being suffers no indifference in any of us. When the sense of material utility and comfort dominates societies with the energy now shown, the results of narrow minds and one-sided culture are especially fatal to the growth of purely ideal occupations. From being an object of love to those who nobly and perseveringly cherish them, they change to an unknown land,

an unexplored region, whose very existence is unsuspected by an immense multitude of the others. Any sort of disinterested thought, of ideal contemplation, of
inward truce, to which the daily newspaper
yields for a moment its dominion, for one
glance that is noble and calm direct from
the heights of reason to things as they
are, will thus remain, in the actual state
of our society, unknown to millions of
minds, minds "educated" and "civilized," who are by our education and customs reduced to the automatism of an
activity that is definitively material. And
more: that kind of servitude should be
held by us the very saddest and lowest of
all the moral conditions we condemn. And
I demand of you that in the battle of life
you defend your souls against that mutilation of them by the tyranny of a single
and self-interested object. Never give, to
either passion or self-interest, but a small
part of what is *you*. For even in material

servitude there is a way to keep free one's inner self, the self of reason and of feeling. So never do you try to justify, by your absorption in labour, in conflict, the enslaving of your soul.

I find in a corner of my memory a story which shall symbolize my meaning. . . . There was a patriarch king, in some far-off Orient where the flock of happy stories has its eyrie; he reigned in a kingdom of that happy candour one finds in Eastern tale; he was called, in man's tradition, the king that was hospitable; immense was his charity. Within its bosom all human misadventure came to end. To it came he who needed bread and he who wanted balsam for a wounded heart. His own reflected, like a sensitive chord, the rhythm of others. His palace was the house of the people. All was liberty and life within that august portal, which never knew a guard; shepherds piped their dances as they waited, old men gossiped while the evening fell, and changing companies of girls replaced the garlands and urns of flowers, flowers which were the only taxes. Merchants of Ophir, traders from Damascus, kept passing through the open gates, competing in showing of rich wares, silks, jewels, perfumes. Before the king's very throne reposed the wearied pilgrim; songbirds attended on his table to pick up crumbs, and at the dawn came little children to tell the king the day had come; as well to souls without fortune as to creatures without soul went out his almsgiving. Nature herself seemed attracted by his largess—the winds, the birds, the very plants, seemed, as in the myth of Orpheus or the legend of Assisi, to seek man's companionship in that oasis of peace. Flowers bloomed unhindered and unplucked in the very paving-stones, twining plants sought the king's own chamber through the open windows; the tired winds laid freely all their scents and

spices o'er his castle; the very spume of
the sea sought to besprinkle its feet; and
the freedom of Paradise, a mighty sharing
of trust, kept up about its walls continual
holy day. . . .

But within—far within, isolated from
the noisy castle by covered passageways,
hidden from the vulgar eye like the lost
chapel of Uhland in the heart of the for-
est, at the end of unknown pathways,
there was a hall of mystery, a home where
no one ventured to set foot save only the
king himself, where even his hospitality
seemed changed to an ascetic egoism. Not
an echo of that external gaiety, not a note
of all that nature-concert, not a word from
the lips of men e'er ventured past the
thickness of those porphyrine sills to move
an air within that forbidden hold. A religious silence brooded on the chastity of
its sleeping air; the light itself gleamed
pale through painted glass, measured into
tint, to fall like a cup of snow in a warm

nest, in heavenly calm. Sometimes, when
the night was clear and still, opening apart
as a shell of pearl, one might see a vision
of the serene shadow. The perfume that
prevailed was that of nenuphar, pure
essence suggestive but of serenity and
thought. Grave caryatides alone guarded
the marble doors, in tranquil pose, the
faces sculptured into profiles grave in introspection. And the old king would assure his people that though no one of
them might accompany him there, his
hospitality prevailed there just as generous, as great, in that mysterious retreat
as ever; only that his guests there bidden
were invisible, impalpable. There he
dreamed, there he freed himself of the
actual, this legendary king; there he
turned his vision inward, smoothed and
refined his thought in meditation like the
pebbles all polished by the wave; there
he bound to the noble forehead the youthful wings of Psyche. . . . And then, at last,

when Death came to remind him that he himself had been but a guest in that palace, the impenetrable house was locked and mute forever ; forever sunken into infinite repose. No one e'er profaned it, no one e'er dared to set irreverent foot within, where the old king had willed to be alone with his dreams, in the solitude of that Thule of his soul.

To this story I liken your inmost kingdom. Open with healthy generosity to all the currents of the world, there exists at the same time, like the secret chamber of that king, an inner forum hidden from all, closed to the common guests, ruled by serene reason alone. Only when you enter within this inviolable sanctuary may you call yourselves free men. They are not free who give up their self-dominion to inordinate affection or selfish interest, forgetting Montaigne's wise precept that our souls may indeed be lent, but never surrendered. To think, to dream, to admire

—these are the ministrants that haunt my cell. The ancients ranked them under the word *otium*, well-employed leisure, which they deemed the highest use of a being truly rational; liberty of thought emancipated of all ignoble chains. Such leisure meant that use of time which they opposed to mere economic activity as the expression of a higher life. Their conception of the dignity of life was linked closely to this lofty conception of leisure; the classical attitude finds its correction and its complement in our modern belief in the dignity of labour; and both employments of one's spirit shall make up a rhythm of individual life whose necessary maintenance needs no insistence on my part. The school of the Stoics which illumined the sunset of antiquity as if with an anticipation of the dawn of Christianity, has left to us a simple but touching image of the salvation of one's inner liberty even in the midst of serfdom in that figure of Cleanto.

Compelled to use his brawny arms in sinking the stones of a fountain or moving a mill wheel, he yet found time to devote the breathing spells of his hard labour to tracing with roughened hand the maxims of Zeno upon the stones. All rational education, all perfect cultivation, of our natures, will take as a starting-point this possibility of rousing in every one of us the double activity which Cleanto's story symbolizes.

Once more; the basic principle of your development, your motto for life, should be to maintain the integrity of your humanity. No one function should ever prevail over that final end. No isolated force can satisfy all reasonable objects of individual existence, as it cannot alone produce the ordered concert of collective existence. And like deformity or dwarfing to the body, is, to the soul, the result of an exclusive object imposed on individual action and a single manner of culture. The falsity of

what is artificial makes ephemeral the
glamour of those societies which have sacrificed the free development of their feeling
or thought, whether to mercantile activity
as in Phœnicia, to wars as in Sparta, to
mysticism as in the terror of the millen-
nium, or to the life of the salon and the
court as in eighteenth century France.

Keep yourselves clear of any mutilation
of your moral nature. Shape the harmonious growth of your spirit for every noble
way; remembering that the most easy,
usual mutilation is that which in human
life as it stands compels a man to forego
this sort of inner life; where all things
high and noble have their being, but, at the
harsh breath of reality, burn in the fires
of an impure passion or wither in the fur-
nace of utilitarianism: the life of which
disinterested meditation is part, and part
the thinking of ideals; that ancient *otium*,
the impenetrable chamber of my story!

And just as the first impulse of profanation will be directed to what is most sacred in the sanctuary, so the common deterioration I would warn you against will begin by your despising what is beautiful. Of all things of the spirit this sense is the most delicate, clear vision of the loveliness of things ; and the one which most quickly withers in a life limited to the invariable round of a vulgar circle, leaving it but a treasured relic abandoned to the care of the few. The emotion for beauty is to the sentiment of other idealities as the jewel to the ring. The effect of a rude touch is as a blow and soon works its fatal work ; and an absolute indifference comes to be in the average soul, where should be perfect love. No stupor of a savage in the presence of the complicated machines of civilization is more intense than the dazed wonder with which too many educated men regard acts which show the intention or the habit of conceding a serious reality to what is beautiful in life.

The argument of the traitor apostle before the jar of ointment, spilled to no practical purpose on the Saviour's head, is
still one of the formulæ of common sense.
The superfluity of art is not, for the name-
less crowd, worth three hundred denarii.
If perchance they respect it, it is as an
esoteric cult. And yet of all the elements
of education that go to make up a full and
noble view of life, surely none more than
Art can justify our interest; for none more
than it includes, as Schiller in eloquent
pages sang, a culture more extensive,
more complete, more fully lending itself
to a concerted stimulus of all the soul's
faculties. Even if the love and admiration
of beauty did not answer of themselves to
a lofty impulse in the rational being, had
not also worth enough to be cultivated for
themselves alone, it would be a motive
highly moral which proposed the culture
of the æsthetic sentiment as a matter of
high interest for all. If to no one it is

given to be without moral sentiment, its education carries with it the duty of preparing the mind for a clear vision also of what is beautiful. Believe me, an educated sense of what is beautiful is the most efficacious collaborator in the forming of a delicate sense of justice. No better instrument exists to dignify, to ennoble the mind. Never does a man more surely fulfil his duty than when he feels it, not as an imposition, but as part of a beautiful harmony. Never will he be a good man more completely than when he knows how to respect in his own work the sentiment of beauty in the others.

Certain it is that the sanctity of goodness purifies and exalts even things of gross exterior. A man may doubtless realize his work without giving it the outward charm of beauty; charity, affection, can become sublime with means that are common, unlovely, even coarse. But it is not only more beautiful, it is greater, that

charity which seeks to transmit itself in
shapes that are delicate and choice, for
then it adds another to its gifts, that sweet,
indescribable lovingness which nothing
can replace and which enhances the gift
with an added light.

To make men see the beautiful is a
work of mercy. Those who demand that
goodness, truth, should ever be shown in
forms that are gloomy and severe, seem
to me to be treasonable to truth and goodness. Virtue itself is an art, a sort of
art divine; smiling, as a mother, on the
Graces. The teacher who would fix in his
scholar's mind the idea that duty is the most
earnest of realities, must at the same time
make him see that it is the highest poetry.
So Guyau, master of lovely comparisons,
uses an incomparable one here: that of
the sculptured saints in some Gothic choir,
each panel matched by one of flowers, so
that for every figure of a saint that shows
his piety or perchance his martyrdom, for

each look divine, each attitude, there corresponds the corolla or the petal of some
flower; to go with the symbolic representa-
tion of good deeds there blossoms, now a
lily, now a rose. So Guyau thinks our
souls should be sculptured; and was not
he himself, the gentle master, in the lovely
evangel of beauty that his genius made, a
living example of that harmony?

I hold it certain that he who has learned
to distinguish the delicate from the common, the ugly from the beautiful, has
gone half the way to knowing the evil
from the good. It is true that mere good
taste is not, as the dilettante might wish,
the only criterion of human actions; yet
one should not, with the narrow ascetic,
consider it a lure to error, a deceitful
guide. We would not indicate it as a certain path to the right; but as a parallel
and near-by road which keeps near to itself the step and vision of the wayfarer.
In the measure that humanity progresses

it sees that the moral law is but beauty of conduct; it shows evil and error like a discord; and will seek for the good as a restored harmony. When the Stoic's severity in Kant inspired the austere words that symbolized his ethics, "He dreamt and thought that life was beauty,—he woke and saw that life was duty," he was not mindful that, although duty may be the supreme reality, in it may also lie the vision of that dream; for consciousness of one's duty, with clear sight of the right, may give it the glamour of beauty too.

In the soul of the redeemer, missionary, or lover of man, must also be required the *understandment of beauty;* there must collaborate with him some elements of the artist's genius. The part played in the efficacy of moral revolutions by the gift of seeing and making known the inner beauty of ideas, is very great. Speaking of the highest of all, it was Renan who said, profoundly: "The poetry of the lesson which makes it loved is more significant than the precept itself, abstractly taken. The originality of the work of Jesus lies not indeed in the literal acceptation of his doctrine—since that might be found entirely without leaving the teachings of the Synagogue, searching for it from the book of Deuteronomy to the Talmud — but in having, by his preaching, made felt the poetry of his precept, that is, its inner beauty."

Dim will be the glory of those epochs or communions which despise the æsthetic bearing of their life or teaching. The Christian asceticism, which only knew how to picture one face of the ideal, excluded from its concept of perfection all which makes life pleasant, refined, beautiful. Its narrow spirit brought it about that man's untamable instinct for liberty, coming back in one of those irresistible reactions of the human spirit, gave birth, in the Italy of the Renaissance, to a type of civilization which considered moral worth a delusion and put faith only in the virtue of a strong or gracious exterior. That Puritanism which persecuted all beauty and all that is select or choice; that shuddered at the chaste nudity of statues; that made a very affectation of what is ugly in its manners, in its dress, in its speech; that sad sect, which, from the English Parliament imposed its will to prohibit all festivities that showed gaiety, and cut any tree that bore flowers — tended, when joined with virtue, to divorce virtue from all thought of beauty. It was a shadow of the tomb of which England has not yet entirely rid itself, which still lasts in the least amiable manifestations of its customs and its religion. Macaulay declared that he preferred the coarse "casket of lead" in which the Puritans guarded their treasure of liberty to the elegant box of carving in which the court of Charles II stored its

refinements. But as neither liberty nor
virtue need be guarded in a casket of lead,
much more for the education of humanity
than all Puritan asceticisms will remain
the grace of the antique ideal, the harmonious teachings of Plato, and that
movement, free and charming, with which
Athens took and lifted to its lips the cup
of life.

The perfection of human morality would
be to cast the spirit of charity in the moulds
of Grecian elegance. And that sweet harmony had once in the world a passing
realization. It was when the word of new-
born Christianity came to Greek colonies
in Macedonia with Saint Paul; to Thessaly and Philippi the Evangel, still pure,
informed the soul of those refined and
spiritual communities, in whom the seal
of Hellenic culture maintained an enchanting native distinction. One might have
hoped then that the two ideals most lofty
that the world had known were going now

to be united for all time. In the epistolary
style of Saint Paul lingers a trace of that
moment when charity was being Hellen-
ized. But that sweet union did not last.
The harmony and serenity of the Pagan
conception of life was left each day more
distant by the new idea which was already
marching to the conquest of the world.
But to conceive of a way in which once
more a step in advance might be shown
for the moral perfectionment of humanity,
one would have to dream that the Christian
ideal again were reconciled with the serene
and luminous joy of ancient times, and
that again the Evangel was being spread
in Philippi and Thessaly.

To cultivate good taste should mean
not only to perfect the external form of
culture, to develop an artistic attitude, and
with exquisite superfluity some elegance
of civilization. Good taste " is the strong
check-rein of the critical judgment."
Martha was able to call it like a second

conscience, which sees us right and brings us back to the light when the first grows obscure or hesitating; and a delicate sense of beauty is for Bagehot as a helpmate of unerring tact in life and of perfect dignity in manners. "The education of good taste," said he, "favours the growth of good sense, which is our necessary viewpoint for the complexities of civilized life. If ever you see such education united in the mind of individuals or societies with any extravagance either of moral or of sentiment, it will be because in such cases it has been cultivated as an isolated, exclusive quality, so rendering impossible the effect of moral perfectionment which it might have brought about in a manner of culture in which no faculty of the mind is developed out of relation to the others."

In a soul which has been the object of harmonious and perfect culture, the inner grace and fineness of the sentiment of the beautiful will be the same thing with

strength and straightness of the reason.
Thus Taine points out that in the grand
works of ancient architecture, beauty is
but sensible manifestation of strength, and
elegance the outer appearance of solidity:
"The same lines of the Parthenon which
delight the view with harmonious propor-
tions, content the intelligence with their
promise of durability."

There is some organic relation, some
natural and close sympathy, which con-
nects the perversions of the will and feeling with the falsities and crudities of bad
taste. If it were given to us to penetrate
into the mysterious labyrinth of the soul,
to reconstruct the intimate story of souls
in the past, in order to discover the formula of their definite moral natures, it
would be an interesting object of study to
determine what, in the refined perversity
of a Nero, corresponds to the germ of a
monstrous histrionism left in the soul of
that sanguinary comedian by the affected

rhetoric of Seneca. And when one calls to mind the oratory of the French Convention and detects a rhetorical perversion everywhere apparent like the feline fur of Jacobinism, it is impossible not to connect like the radii that part from one centre, like the signs of an identical insanity, the extravagance of taste, the vertigo of all moral sentiment, and the fanatical limitation of the reason.

Undoubtedly there is no more certain result of the æsthetic sense than that which teaches us to distinguish as relative the good and the true and the beautiful, and accept some possibility of beauty in evil and error. Yet one need not neglect this truth, definitively true, by believing in some sympathetic connection between all these lofty objects of the soul and considering each one of them as but the starting-point, not the only one, but still one, whence it is possible to go to a meeting with the others.

The notion, then, of a higher accord between good taste and the moral sense is therefore true, as well in the spirit of individuals as of societies. For what concerns these last, that accord may have its example in the relation affirmed by Rosenkranz to exist between liberty and the moral order, on the one hand, and the beauty of the human form which results from the development of races, on the other. That typical beauty reflects, for the Hegelian thinker, the ennobling effect of liberty; for slavery makes ugly at the same time that it degrades, while the consciousness of their harmonious development impresses the outward seal of beauty on races that are free.

In the characters of peoples, the gifts derived from fine taste, the mastery of gracious form, the delicate power to interest, the virtue of making ideas likeable, go with the genius of propaganda—that is to say, the mighty gift of universality.

Certain it is that to the possession of these chosen attributes may be referred the meaning of the word *human*, which the French spirit is quick to apply to all it chooses out and commends. Ideas grow strong and speedy wings, not in the cold bosom of abstractions, but in the warm and luminous air of actual shape. Their superior diffusion, their greater prevalence at times, result because the Graces have bathed them in their light. And just so, in the evolution of life itself, those enchanting outward signs of nature which in seeming represent only the gift of superfluous caprice — music, the painted plumage of birds, the corolla of flowers, their perfume — are as advertisement to the insect that bears the fecund pollen. They have played, amid the elements of the struggle for life, a function of great realism, in that, showing a superior motive, a reason for preference, to the love instinct, they have caused to survive in every species those beings that are best endowed with beauty over all the others.

For one who has instinctive love of beauty, there is indeed a certain kind of mortification in stooping to defend it by arguments that are based on any other reason or principle than that impossible and disinterested love for it which satisfies a fundamental impulse of any rational being. But unfortunately this motive has lost its empire over a vast number of men, to whom it is necessary to teach a due respect for a love they do not share by showing them what are the relations which connect it with other classes of human interest. And to do this one must often cope with a vulgar view of such relations: that anything that tends to soften the outlines of the social character or customs and sharpens the sense of beauty, to make of taste a delicate sensibility of the soul and of grace the universal form of action is (for such critics, disciples of the harsh and useful only) to depreciate all that is heroic, virile in the temper of society, on the one hand, and its positive utilitarian capacity on the other. In "The Toilers of the Sea" we read how the people of Jersey when they first saw a steamboat anathematized it on account of the tradition that fire and water are hostile elements; the common *critique* abounds with beliefs in similar enmities. If you propose to make common love of the beautiful, you must begin by making men understand the possibility of harmonic concert between all legitimate human activities; and that will be an easier task than to convert them straightway to a love of the beautiful, in itself. To make the mass of men unwilling to expel the swallows from the home, one must, as Pythagoras counselled, first convince them —not of the gracefulness of the bird or its legendary virtue—but that its nests will in no manner interfere with the durability of the shingles or tiles where they build!

To that conception of human life which is formed on the free and harmonious development of our nature, and therefore includes among its essential objects the satisfaction of our feeling for the beautiful, is opposed—as a rule for human conduct—the conception called utilitarian, under which our whole activities are governed by their relation to the immediate ends of self-interest. The blame of a narrow utilitarianism as the only monitor of the spirit of our century, meted out to it in the name of the ideal with all the rigours of Anathema, is based in part in the failure to recognize that its Titanic efforts for the subordination of the forces of Nature to the human will and for the extension of material well-being are a necessary labour to prepare, as by the laborious enrichment of an exhausted soil, for the flowering of future idealisms. The transitory predominance of that function of utility which has absorbed the agitated and feverish life of the last hundred years with its most potent energies explains, however, although it does not justify, many of the painful yearnings, many discontents and grievances of the intelligence, which show themselves either by a melancholy and exalted idealization of the past, or by a cruel despair of the future. For this there is one fruitful and well-adventured thought in the proposition of a certain group of thinkers of these last generations, among whom I need only cite again the noble figure of Guyau, who have tried to seal the definitive reconciliation of the conquests of the century with the renovation of many old human devotions, and have put into this blessed work as many treasures of love as of genius.

Often you will have heard attributed to two main causes that torrent of the spirit of utility which gives its note to the moral physiognomy of the present century, with its neglect of the æsthetic and disinterested view of life. The revelations of natural science, whose interpreters, favourable or the reverse, agree in destroying all ideality for its base, are one; the other is the universal diffusion and triumph of democratic ideas. I propose to speak to you exclusively of this latter cause; because I trust that your first initiation in the revelations of Science has been so directed as to preserve you from the danger of a vulgar interpretation. Upon democracy weighs the accusation of guiding humanity, by making it mediocre, to a Holy Empire of Utilitarianism. This accusation is reflected with vibrant intensity in the pages—for me always full of a suggestive charm—of the most amiable among the masters of the Modern Spirit: the seductive pages of Renan, to whose authority you have often heard me refer and of whom I may often speak again. Read Renan, those of you who have not done so already, and you will have to love him as I do. No one as he, among the moderns, appears to me such a master "of that art of teaching with Grace" which Anatole France considers divine. No one so well as he has succeeded in combining irony with pity; even in the rigour of the analysis he can put the unction of the priest. And even when he teaches us to doubt, his exquisite gentleness sheds a balsam over the doubt itself. His thoughts ring in our minds with echoes ineffable, so vague as to remind one of sacred music. His infinite comprehension makes critics class him among those dilettantes of a light scepticism who wear the gown of the philosopher like the domino of a mask ; but, once you penetrate his spirit, you will see that the vulgar tolerance of the mere sceptic differs from his as the hospitality of a worldly *salon* from the real spirit of charity.

This master holds, then, that high preoccupation with the ideal interests of our race is irreconcilable with the spirit of democracy. He believes that the conception of life in a society where that spirit dominates will gradually come to seek only material welfare, as the good most attainable for the greatest number. According to him, democracy is the enthronement of Caliban. Ariel can but be vanquished by its triumph. Many others who most care for æsthetic culture and select spirit are of a like mind. Thus Bourget thinks that universal triumph of democratic institutions will make civilization lose in profundity what it gains in extension. He sees its necessary end in the empire of individual mediocrity. "Who says democracy voices the evolution of individual tendencies and the devolution of culture." These judgments have a lively interest for us Americans who love the cause and consequence of that Revolution which in our America is entwined with the glory of its origin, and believe instinctively in the possibility of a noble and rare individual life which need never sacrifice its dignity to the caprices of the rabble. To confront the problem one must first recognize that if democracy do not uplift its spirit by a strong ideal interest which it shares with its preoccupation by material interests, it does lead, and fatally, to the favouring of mediocrity, and lacks, more than any other social system, barriers within which it may safely seek the higher culture. Abandoned to itself, without the constant rectification of some active moral sanction which shall purify and guide its motives to the dignifying of life—democracy will, gradually, extinguish the idea of any superiority which may not be turned into a more efficient training for the war of interests. It is then the most ignoble form of the brutalities of power. Spiritual preference, exaltation of life by unselfish motive, good taste and art and manners, and the admiration of all that is worthy and of good repute, will then alike vanish unprotected when social equality has destroyed all grades of excellence without replacing them with others that shall also rule by moral influence and the light of reason.

Any equality of conditions in the order of society, like homogeneity in nature, is but an unstable equilibrium. From that moment when democracy shall have worked its perfect work of negation by the levelling of unjust superiorities, the equality so won should be but a starting-point. Its affirmation remains; and the affirmation of democracy and its glory consist in arousing in itself by fit incentives the revelation and the mastery of the true superiorities of men.

With relation to the conditions of the life of America, that duty of attaining the true conception of our social state is doubly needful. Our democracies grow rapidly by the continual addition of a vast cosmopolitan multitude, by a stream of immigration which is merged with a nucleus already too weak to make active effort at assimilation and so contain the human flood by those dikes which an ancient solidity of social structure can alone provide, a secured political order, and the elements of a culture that has become deeply rooted. This rapid growth exposes our future to the dangers of a democratic degeneration which smothers under the blind force of the mass all idea of quality, deprives the social consciousness of all just notion of order, and, yielding its class organization to the rough hands of chance, causes the triumph of only the most ignoble, unjustifiable supremacies.

It is, of course, true that our selfish advantage—not the virtue of it alone—bids us be hospitable. Long since the need of peopling the emptiness of the desert made a famous publicist coin the phrase, "To govern is to populate." But this fa-

mous aphorism contains a truth that must
not be closely interpreted; it must not
ascribe civilizing virtues to mere number.
To govern is to populate by assimilation,
first of all, and then by education and
selection. If the appearance and growth
in a society of the highest human activities require a dense population, it is pre-
cisely because great numbers make possible the most complete division of labour,
and the birth of elements of strong leadership which bring about the predominance
of quality over quantity. The multitude,
the anonymous mass, is nothing by itself.
It will be an instrument of barbarity or of
civilization according as it has or lacks
the coefficient of high moral leadership.
There is deep truth in Emerson's paradox
that every country on earth should be
judged by its minorities and not its majorities. The civilization of a country
acquires its grandeur, not by its manifestations of material prosperity and predomi-

nance, but by the higher order of thinking
or of feeling made thereby possible. So
Comte : it is senseless to pretend that excellence can ever be replaced by number,
that by an accumulation of vulgar minds
one may hit upon a brain of genius, or by
the addition of many mediocre virtues get
the equivalent of a deed of heroism. So
our democracy, proclaiming the universality and equality of rights, will sanction
the ignoble predominance of mere number
unless it be careful highly to maintain the
idea of human superiorities that are legitimate ; and to make authority, bound to a
popular vote, not the exponent of an absolute equality, but (as I remember some
young Frenchman said) ''the consecration
of a hierarchy based on liberty.''

The clash between the democratic rule
and the higher life becomes a fatal reality
when that rule imparts the disregard of
even legitimate superiorities and the sub-
stitution of mechanical government for a

faith in heroism (in Carlyle's sense). All
in civilization that is more than material
excellence, economic prosperity, is a height
that will be levelled when moral authority
is given to the average mind. Though
there be no longer external invading hordes
to hurl themselves upon the beacon lights
of civilization with a might now devastat-
ing and now regenerating, the high culture of to-day should guard itself against
the soft and gradual dissolvent work of
those other crowds, pacific, even educated
—the unescapable multitudes of the vulgar, whose Attila might well be personi-
fied in "Mr. Homais," whose heroism is
shrewdness, ordered by an instinctive re-
pugnance for what is great; whose device
is the leveller. Immovable indifference and
quantitative superiority are its attributes,
the usual result of its labours; yet is it not
entirely incapable of rising to epic heights,
usually of anger, giving free reins to its
antipathies. Charles Morice called it "those

phalanxes of ferocious Prudhommes who have for their device Mediocrity, and march together in their hatred of all that is extra-ordinary.''

Elevated to power, these Prudhommes will make of their triumphant will an organized hunting-party against all that shows aptitude or daring wing to fly high. Its social formula will be a democracy which leads to the consecration of Pope Anyone, the coronation of King Average. They will hate merit as a rebellion. In their dominion all noble superiority will be like a marble statue placed in a miry road to be spattered by the mud of any passing waggon. They will call the dog-matism of common sense, wisdom; mean avidness of heart, gravity; adaptation to the mediocre, sound judgment; and bad taste, manly indifference to trifles. Their notion of justice will lead them either to substitute in history the immortality of great men by the common forgetfulness of all, or to preserve it with the equal memory of a Mithridates who knew the names of all his soldiers. Its manner of republicanism will resemble that of Fox, who used to submit his projects to the criterion of that member who seemed to him the most perfect type of the country gentleman, judging by the limitation of his faculties and the rudeness of his gestures. Then we shall be in that Zoöcracy that Baudelaire imagined, and Shakespeare's Titania, kissing an ass's head, will be the emblem of that liberty which calls but for the middling. Never could a tyrant's conquest compass a more sinister end!

And if you make a prophet of your neighbour who preaches the belittling lesson of the mediocre, if you make him your hero and seek your salvation in his bureaucratic content—you will encounter that rancorous, implacable hostility against all that is beautiful, all that is dignified or delicate in the spirit of humanity which, even more than its brutal shedding of blood, is so repugnant in the Jacobite tyranny. Before its tribunal the wisdom of a Lavoisier, the genius of a Chenier, the dignity of a Malesherbes, become only faults; amid the shouting of its Conventions we hear the cry, Distrust that man, he has written a book! Confounding the idea of democratic simplicity with Rousseau's state of nature, it would take the vignette of his first edition as symbolic of the antinomy between democracy and culture, that famous diatribe against the arts and sciences in the name of morality; a satyr, rudely seizing the torch of Prometheus from his hands, only to learn that its flame is mortal to him who touches it!

Equalitarian ferocity has not, indeed, yet shown itself in the democratic development of our century, nor opposed in brutal manner the serenity and liberty of our intellectual growth. But like some savage beast now domesticated, its later

progeny have changed their native ferocity
to an artful and ignoble tameness, equalitarianism; and this mild tendency to all
that is utilitarian or vulgar may fairly be
blamed upon the democracy of the nine-
teenth century. No sensitive or sagacious
mind has ever studied this without anx-
iously considering some of its results in
their social and their political aspect.
Contemporary thought, while rejecting
that false conception of equality that made
the delirium of the French Revolution, has
yet maintained a severe scrutiny of the
very theory of democracy, which you, who
are about to create the future, must begin
with; not necessarily to upset, but to educate, the spirit of our time.

Since our century began to assume independence, personal liberty in the evolution of its ideas, German idealist philosophy has rectified the equalitarian Utopia
of the eighteenth century and again exalted, albeit with too much Cæsarism, the

part played in history by individual greatness. Comte's positivism, not recognizing
in the democratic equality anything but a
transitory wiping out of ancient class sys-
tems, and denying with equal conviction
the definitive efficiency of popular rule,
sought in the principles of natural classification a basis for that social classification
which should be the substitute for the
hierarchies recently destroyed. The criti-
cism of the democratic régime took a
severer form in the generation of Taine
and Renan : to this modern Athenian the
only equality which appealed was one like
that of Athens, "an equality of demigods."
And as to Taine, he wrote "the Origin of
contemporary France"; and if, on the
one hand, his conception of society as an
organism leads him logically to reject all
idea of uniformity opposed to the principles of dependent and subordinate organ-
isms, on the other his fine instinct for
intellectual selection leads him to abomi-

nate the invasion of the heights by the
multitude. Already the great voice of Carlyle had preached against irreverent levelling, and for heroism; meaning by that
word any noble superiority; and Emerson
echoed this idea in the bosom of the most
positivist of democracies. The new science spoke of natural selection as a necessity of all progress; and in art, where the
feeling for the exquisite has its most obvious application, those notes reverberated
which seek to express the feeling of what
we may call the estrangement of the spirit
to modern conditions of life. Nor to hear
them is it necessary to copy that Parnas-
sian spirit of a delicate and feeble stock
which an aristocratic disdain for the present drives to reclusion in the past. Of the
constant inspirations of Flaubert — from
whom springs directly the most democra-
tized of all the modern schools — none is
more intense than his hatred for a mediocrity animated by the spirit of levelling

and the tyranny of mass. And within contemporary Scandinavian literature, so much preoccupied by social questions, the same idea most often occurs. Ibsen weaves the lofty harangue of his Stockmann upon the affirmation that "compact majorities are the greatest danger to liberty and truth." And the awesome Nietzsche opposes to the ideal of a mediatized humanity that of supermen who surge above its level like a tidal wave. A lively desire for a reform of the social system which shall make secure the leading of the heroic life and assure to its thought a purer atmosphere of dignity and just consideration is now everywhere apparent, and promises to be a fundamental note in the harmonies of the coming century.

Yet the spirit of democracy is essentially, for our civilization, a principle against which it were idle to rebel. The discontent we feel for the imperfections of its actual historic *form* has often led us to

judge unjustly what it has that is both
final and fruitful. Thus Renan's wisdom
of the aristocrat it is which formulates the
most explicit condemnation of its fundamental principle, equality of rights, which
he believes to be permanently contrary
to any possible government of intellectual
superiority. He even goes so far as to call
it, in a forceful image, "the antipodes of
the path of God — since God has not willed
that all should live in the same degree of
spiritual life." These unjust paradoxes,
together with his famous ideal of an omnipotent oligarchy of wise men, are like
the exaggerated image in a nightmare of
some true thought that has obsessed our
waking hours. Failure to recognize the real
work of democracy because it has not yet
succeeded in reconciling its principle of
equality with social safeguards for that of
selection, is as to ignore the parallel labour
of science because, when interpreted in the
narrow manner of a certain school, it has

occasionally wrought harm to the spirit of poetry or religion. Democracy and science are indeed the two props on which our civilization rests, the two Fates that spin our future; as Bourget phrases it, "In them we are, we live, we move." As it is impossible, therefore, to hope with Renan for a more positive consecration of the moral superiorities, the realization of a hierarchy of reason, any effective dominion of the loftier gifts of intelligence and free will which shall be based on the destruction of that democratic equality,—the only thing left us is to bethink us how to educate, reform, democracy itself. We must seek how gradually to inculcate in popular feeling and custom the idea of that necessary subordination, the sense of true superiorities, the instinctive yet conscious cultivation of all that multiplies the cipher of human worth in the eye of reason.

Popular education thus acquires its su-

preme interest considered in its relation to
such a work, and with thought for the
future.[1] And it is at school where we first
mould the clay of the multitude; there
come the first and broadest manifestations
of social equity; schools consecrated to the
equal right of all to learning and the most
efficient measures for superior attainment.
They have to round out a noble task — to
make the sense for order and the will for
justice prime objects of its instruction; the
realization of all that Authority which is
legitimate.

There is no distinction more easily lost
sight of in the popular mind than that between equality of opportunity and actual
equality — of influence or of power —
among members of organized society. All
have the same right to aspire to a moral
superiority which may justify and explain

[1] " Plus l'instruction se répand, plus elle doit faire de part aux
idées générales et généreuses. On croit que l'instruction populaire
doit être terre-à-terre. C'est le contraire qui est la vérité." —
Fouillée : *L'Idée moderne du droit*, Libre, 5, IV.

an effective one; but only those who have really achieved the former should be rewarded by the latter. The true and worthy notion of equality rests on the assumption that all reasonable beings are endowed by nature with faculties capable of a noble development. The duty of the State consists in seeing that all its members are so placed as to be able to seek without favour their own *best;* in so arranging things as to bring to light each human superiority, wherever it exists. In such wise, after the initial equality, inequality, when it comes, will be justified; for it will be sanctioned either by the mysterious powers of nature or the deserving merit of volition. So understood, democratic equality, far from antagonizing a choice of either customs or ideas, will become the useful instrument of that spiritual election, the native soil for culture. For it is born of intellectual energy; as Tocqueville said, poesy and eloquence, the graces of the mind, the flashes of the imagination, all these gifts of the soul, scattered from the heavens at hazard, are co-workers in the labour of democracy and serve it even when they belong to its enemies; for they tend to bring into relief the natural — not the inherited — greatness of which man's spirit is capable. Emulation, the most powerful spur of all that urge to action, as well in thought as in other human activities, needs as well equality at the starting-point in order to produce at the finish that inequality which gives the palm to the apter scholar or the greater man. And the democratic régime can carry in its bosom both these two conditions of emulation only when it does not degenerate into a levelling equality, but is content to look forward to it only as a glorious ideal, a counsel of perfection, a future equality of all men in their common ascent to the highest culture possible.

Rationally conceived, democracy always admits that indispensable aristocratic principle which shall concede superiority to the better man when recognized and sanctioned by the common consent. It consecrates, as much as aristocracy, the distinction of equality; but it resolves in favour of such qualities as are truly superior — those of mind, character, virtue. It does not immobilize them into a separate class which shall have the execrable privilege of caste, but renews them continually from the living fountain of the people, making justice or affection the reason of their choice. In such wise recognizing, as a necessity for any progress, the selection and predominance of the best equipped, it avoids that humiliation which in other human contests falls to the lot of the vanquished. "The great law of natural selection will go on functioning in human society only so long as it works more and more on a basis of liberty," said Fouillée. The odious character of traditional aristocracies arose in that they were oppressive

in their action and unjust in their founda-
tion, and so their authority became intoler-
able. Now we know that there exists no
other legitimate limit for man's equality
than that which consists in the dominion
of intelligence and virtue, freely consented
to by all.

But we do know that it is necessary that
this limit shall exist. On the other hand,
our Christian view of life teaches that those
moral superiorities which are the basis of
rights really give rise only to duties; and
that each superior being owes to others
more in proportion to his excess in ability
over them. The anti-equality views of
Nietzsche, who seems to have ploughed so
deep a furrow in our contemporary literature of thought, have brought into his tre-
mendous revindication of what he calls
natural rights, implicit in human superiorities, an abominable and reactionary
genius. For, in scoffing at all mercy, all
fraternity, he places in the heart of the su-

perman he deifies a Satanic disregard of the weak and the disinherited; he legitimizes all privileges of self-will and force to governments of the gibbet and the lash, and with logical resolution comes to his keynote: "Society does not exist for itself, but for its elect." Truly it is not this monstrous notion that we oppose as our standard to that false equalitarianism which aims at the levelling of all to a common vulgarity. Happily, so long as there shall be in our world the possibility of so disposing two pieces of wood that they form a Cross — which is to say, eternally — so long shall future man persist in thinking that it is Love that is the basis of all stable order; and that the only true hierarchy is that of those who have the highest capacity for love.

The new science — a fountain of inexhaustible moral inspirations — shows, in explaining life's laws, how the principle of democracy may be reconciled with an

aristocracy of morals or of culture in the
organization of human collectivities. On
the one hand, as Henri Bérenger's suggestive book has shown, the affirmations
of science but contribute to sanction and
fortify the idea of democracy in society,
revealing how great is the value of collective effort, how valuable the labour even of
the smallest hand, how immense the field
of action reserved to the anonymous and
obscure fellow-workman in any manifestation of our social evolution. It exalts, no
less than Christianity, the dignity of the
lowly ; this new thought, which in nature
ascribes to the labour of the infinitely little,
the nummulite and the briozoön at the
depths of the ocean, the construction of the
cements of geology ; which derives from
the vibration of a formless primitive cell
all the elevating impulses of organized life;
which shows the great rôle that in our
psychology we must ascribe to vague and
inconspicuous phenomena, even the fugi-

tive perceptions of our subconscious self; and which, coming to sociology and history, restores to the heroism of the masses, often doubted, the share which was ignored in the glorification of the individual hero; and reveals the slow accumulation of individual research which through many centuries has prepared, in obscure workshops or laboratories of forgotten toilers, the discoveries of genius.

But at the same time that it thus demonstrates the immortal efficacy of collective force, and dignifies the participation of unknown collaborators in the universal work, science shows that it is a necessary condition to all progress that there should be leadership amid the immense mass of persons and of things. Relations of dependence and subordination are a condition of life, between the individual members of society and the elements of individual organization. In fine, there is an inherent necessity for the universal law of imitation that there be present models, alive and influential, for the making perfect human society, to realize their superiority by the progressive making general of it.

To show how both these universal lessons of science can be transformed into action, working together in the organization and spirit of society, we need only insist on our conception of a democracy that is just and noble, impelled only by the knowledge and sense of true superiorities, in which the supremacy of intelligence and virtue, the only limits to the just equality of men, receives its authority and prestige from liberty and sheds over all multitudes the beneficent aura of love. And at the same time that it reconciles these two great lessons, of our observation of the order of nature, such a society will realize the harmony of two historic forces which give our civilization its essential character, its regulative principles of life. From the spirit of Christianity, in fact, is born the sentiment of equality, albeit tainted now with something of the ascetic disdain for culture and selection of the spirit. And from the classic civilizations rises that sense for order, for authority, and the almost religious respect for genius, though tainted with something of aristocratic disdain for the weak and the lowly. The future shall synthesize these two suggestions in immortal formula; then shall Democracy have triumphed definitely. Democracy — which, when threatening an ignoble levelling, justifies the lofty protests and the bitter melancholies of those who see sacrificed in her triumph all intellectual distinction, every dream of art, each delicacy of life, — will, now even more than the old aristocracies, extend inviolable guaranties for the cultivation of those flowers of the soul which fade and perish in the surroundings of the vulgar, amid the pitiless tumult of the multitude.

The utilitarian conception as the idea of human destiny, and equality at the mediocre as the norm of social proportion; make up the formula which in Europe they call the spirit of Americanism. It is impossible to think on either of these as inspirations for human conduct or society, while contrasting them with those which are opposed to them, without at once conjuring up by association a vision of that formidable and fruitful democracy there in the North, with its manifestations of prosperity and power, as a dazzling example in favour of the efficacy of democratic institutions and the correct aim of its ideas. If one could say of utilitarianism that it is the word of the English spirit, the United States may be considered the incarnation of that word. Its Evangel is spread on every side to teach the material miracles of its triumph. And Spanish America is not wholly to be entitled, in its relation to the United States, as a nation of Gentiles. The mighty confederation is realizing over us a sort of moral conquest. Admiration for its greatness, its strength, is a sentiment that is growing rapidly in the minds of our governing classes, and even more, perhaps, among the multitude, easily impressed with victory or success. And from admiring it is easy to pass to imitating. Admiration and belief are already for the psychologist but the passive mood of imitation. "The imitative tendency of our moral nature," says Bagehot, "has its seat in that part of the soul where lives belief." Common sense and experience would suffice of themselves to show this natural relation. We imitate him in whose superiority and prestige we believe. So it happens that the vision of a voluntarily delatinized America, without compulsion or conquest, and regenerate in the manner of its Northern archetype, floats already through the dreams of many who are sincerely interested in our future, satisfies them with suggestive parallels they find at every step, and appears in constant movements for reform or innovation. We have our *mania for the North.* It is necessary to oppose to it those bounds which both sentiment and reason indicate.

Not that I would make of those limits an absolute negation. I well understand that enlightenment, inspiration, great lessons lie in the example of the strong; nor do I fail to realize that intelligent attention to the claims of the material and the study of the useful, directed abroad, is of especially useful result in the case of people in the formative stage, whose nationality is still in the mould. I understand how one must try by persevering education to rectify such traits of a society as need to be made to fit in with new demands of civilization and new opportunities in life, thus by wise innovation counteracting the forces of heredity or custom. But I see no good in denaturalizing the character of a people

— its personal genius — to impose on it
identity with a foreign model to which
they will sacrifice the originality of their
genius, that, once lost, can never be replaced; nor in the ingenuous fancy that
this result may ever be obtained artifi-
cially or by process of imitation. That
thoughtless attempt to transplant what is
natural and spontaneous in one society into
the soil of another where it has no roots,
historically or naturally, seemed to Michelet like the attempt to incorporate by mere
transference a dead organism in a living
body.

In societies, as in art or literature, blind
imitation gives but an inferior copy of the
model. And in the vain attempt there is
also something ignoble; a kind of political
snobbery, carefully to copy the ways and
acts of the great; as, in Thackeray's satire,
those without rank or fortune ineffectually
imitate only the foibles of the mighty.
Care for one's own independence, per-

sonality, judgment, is a chief form of self-respect. A much-commented passage of Cicero teaches how it is our duty sedulously to preserve our original character; that which differentiates and determines, so far as may wisely be, the primal natural impulses, as they derive from a various distribution of natural gifts and so make up the concert and the order of the world. And even more would this seem to be true as applied to human collectivities. But perhaps you will say that there is no seal, no peculiar and definite thing to mark the quality for whose permanence and integrity we should do battle in the actual organization of our people. Perhaps there lacks in our South American character the definite contour of a personality. But even so, we Latin-Americans have an inheritance of Race, a great ethnic tradition to maintain, a sacred bond which unites us to immortal pages of history and puts us on our honour to preserve this for the future. That cosmopolitanism which **we** have to respect as the irresistible tendency of our development need not exclude that sentiment of fidelity to the past, nor that moulding and directing force of which the genius of our race must avail itself in the fusing of the elements that shall constitute the American of the future.

It has more than once been pointed out that the great epochs of history, its most fertile periods, are always the result of distinct but coexisting forces which by their very agreement to oppose maintain the interest and stimulus of life, which in the quietism of a universal accord might tend to disappear. So the two extremes of Athens and Sparta revolve on an axle around which circles the race of greatest genius man has known. So America needs at this time to maintain its original duality, which has converted from classic myth to actual history the story of the two eagles, loosed at the same moment from either

pole, to arrive at the same moment at each
one's limit of dominion. This difference
in genius does not exclude honourable
emulation, nor discourage in very many
relations agreement or even solidarity.
And if one can dimly foresee even a higher
concord in the future, that will be due not
to a one-sided imitation of one race by the
other, but to a reciprocity of influences and
a skilful harmonizing of those attributes
which make the peculiar glory of either
race.

Still, the dispassionate study of that
civilization which some would offer to us
as a model, affords a reason no less potent
than those which are based only on the in-
dignity and unworthiness of mere imitation to temper the enthusiasm of those who
propose it as our model. . . . And now I
come to the very theme of my discourse,
and the relation to it of this spirit of imitation. Any severe judgment formed upon
our neighbours of the North should begin,

like the courteous fencer, by lowering a
rapier in salute to them. Easy is this for
me. Failure to recognize their faults does
not seem to me so insensate as to deny
their qualities. Born — to employ Beau-
delaire's paradox — with the innate experience of liberty, they have kept themselves faithful to the law of their birth;
and have developed, with the precision and
certainty of a mathematical progression,
the fundamental principles of their organization. This gives to their history a unity
which, even if it has excluded the acquire-
ment of different aptitudes or merits, has
at least the intellectual beauty of being logical. The traces of its progress will never be
expunged from the annals of human right,
because they have been the first to evoke
our modern ideal of liberty and to convert
it from the uncertainty of experiment and
the visions of Utopia into imperishable
bronze and living reality. For they have
shown by their example the possibility of

extending the immovable authority of a republic over an immense national commonwealth, and, with their federal organization, have revealed — as de Tocqueville
felicitously put it — the manner in which
the brilliancy and power of great states
may be combined with the felicity and
peace of little ones. . . .

Theirs are many of the most daring
deeds for which the perspective of time
shall distinguish this century ; theirs is the
glory of having revealed completely the
greatness and dignity of labour, thereby
accentuating the firmest note of moral
beauty in all our civilization ; that blest
force which antiquity abandoned to the
abjection of slavery, and which to-day we
identify with the highest expression of human dignity, based on the consciousness
and the exertion of its own merit. Strong,
tenacious of purpose, holding inaction as
opprobrious, they have placed in the
hands of the mechanic of their shops and

the farmer of their fields the mystic key of
Hercules, and have given to human genius a new and unwonted beauty, girding
it with the leathern apron of the hand-
worker. Each one of these presses on to
conquer life as his Puritan ancestors did
the wilderness. Persistent followers of that
creed of individual energy which makes
of every man the artificer of his destiny,
they have modelled their commonwealth
on a kind of imaginary population of Cru-
soes, who, as soon as they have roughly
attended to their training in the art of
taking care of themselves, will turn to the
making of themselves into a stable State.
And, never sacrificing to this their conception of the sovereign Individual, they yet
have known how at the same time to make
of their association the most admirable instrument of their grandeur and empire;
they have got from the sum of their energies, as devoted to research, industry,
philanthropy, results that are the more

marvellous in that they were secured with
the most absolute integrity of their personal liberty.

They have a sleepless and insatiable instinct of curiosity, an impatient eagerness
for the light; and, carrying a fondness
for public education almost to the point
of monomania, have made the common
school the surest prop of their prosperity,
believing that the mind of the child should
be the most cherished of their precious
things. Their culture, while far from
being spiritual or refined, has an admirable
efficiency so far as it is directed to practical
ends and their immediate realization. And,
while they have not added to the acquisi-
tions of science a single general law, one
new principle, they have done wonders in
its application to new inventions and made
giant strides in its service to utilities; in
the steam boiler, the electric dynamo, are
now billions of invisible slaves who centuple for their Aladdin the power of the

magic lamp. The growth of their greatness and power will astonish future generations. By their marvellous gift for im-
provisation they have found a spur to time,
so that in a few years they conjure, as it
were from a desert, the fruitage hitherto
the work of centuries.

And that Puritan liberty which gave
them light in the past unites with that
light a piety which still endures. Beside
the factory and the school it has erected
churches whence ascend the prayers of
millions of free consciences. They have
been able to save from the shipwreck of
all the idealities that which is the highest of all, and kept alive the tradition
of a religious sentiment which, if it does
not uplift on wings of the highest idealism, spirituality, at least maintains over
the utilitarian stampede some rein of the
moral sense. Also, they have known how
to maintain a certain primitive robustness
even amidst the refinements of a highly

civilized life; they hold to the pagan cult of health, sanity, and strength; they preserve in strong muscles the instrument of a strong will; obliged by their insatiable ambition to employ all human energies, they fit the torso of the athlete over the heart of the free man. And from all this springs a dominant note of optimism, confidence, faith, which makes them face the future with a proud and stubborn assurance; the note of "Excelsior" and the "Psalm of Life," which their poets have opposed as a balsam to melancholy or bitterness of spirit.

Thus it is that their Titanic greatness impresses even those made most distrustful by their exaggerations of character and the recent violences of their history; and I, who do not love them, as you see, admire them still. I admire them, first, for their formidable power of *desire;* I bow before that "*school of will and work*" — which Philarete Chasles tells us they have inherited from their forbears.

In the beginning was Action. With these
famous words of Faust the future historian
of the great Republic may begin; the
Genesis, not yet concluded, of their national existence. Their genius may be defined as the universe of the *Dynamists:*
force in movement. Above all, it has the
capacity, the enthusiasm, the fortunate
vocation, for doing things; volition is the
chisel which has shapen this people from
hard rock. Their characteristic points are
manifestations of the will-power, originality, and audacity. Their history is
above all a very paroxysm of virile activity. Their typical figure should be entitled,
not Superman, but He who wants. And if
anything saves them collectively from vulgarity, it is that extraordinary *verve* of
energy which they always show and which
lends a certain epic character to even the
struggles of self-interest and the material
life. So Bourget could say, of the specu-
lators of Minneapolis and Chicago that

they are of the mould of gladiators, that
their fighting power of attack or of defence
is as of Napoleon's soldiers of the Guard.
Yet that supreme energy with which the
North American seems to cast, as if by
hypnotizing, a spell and suggestion over
the Fates, is found only in just those things
which are presented to us as exceptional,
divergent, in their civilization. No one will
say that Edgar Poe was not an anomalous
individual, rebellious to the influences
around him : his chosen spirit represented
a particle inassimilable by the national
soul, which vainly struggled to express itself to others as from an infinite solitude;
yet the fundamental note — Baudelaire has
pointed it out — in the character of Poe's
heroes is still the inner shrine, the uncon-
querable resistance of the will. When he
imagined Ligeia, most mysterious and
adorable of his creatures, he symbolized
in the inextinguishable light of her eyes
the hymn of the triumph of man's will
over death.

If now by a sincere recognition of what is great and brilliant in the genius of that mighty country I have acquired the right to complete the picture by meting even-handed justice, one question, full of interest, still presents itself: Does that society realize or at least tend to realize, the ideal of such rational conduct as satisfies, to the heart's desire, the intellectual and moral dignity of our civilization? Is it there that we shall find the most approximate image of our perfect State? That feverish unrest which seems to centuple in its bosom the movement, the intensity of life — has it an end that is worth while and a motive sufficient for its justification?

Herbert Spencer, when with a noble sincerity he framed his parting address to the democracy of America at a New York banquet, marked as the chief feature of North American life that same overflowing unrest which shows itself both in the infinite passion for work and in vainglory in all forms of material expansion. Later he said that so exclusive a preoccupation with those activities which make for immediate utility revealed a notion of life, tolerable indeed in a young country as a provisional stage of civilization, but which already needed rectifying as it tended to make "useful" labor the end and object of all living; whereas in no case can it mean more than the accumulation of those things which are only the necessary elements to a full and harmonious development of our being. And he added that it behooved them now to teach their people the gospel of rest or recreation; and we, identifying these words with the *otium* of the ancients, will include in this gospel to be taught those restless toilers *any* ideal concern, *any* disinterested employment of one's time, *any* object of meditation or study divorced from all relation to immediate utilitarian interest.

North American life, indeed, describes

that vicious circle which Pascal remarked in the ceaseless seeking for well-being when it has no object outside of oneself. Its prosperity is as immense as its incapability of satisfying even a mediocre view of human destiny. Titanic in its enormous concentration of human will-power, in its unprecedented triumph in all spheres of material aggrandizement, its civilization yet produces as a whole a singular impression of insufficiency, of emptiness. And if man's spirit demands, with all the reason that thirty centuries of growth under classic and under Christian influence have conferred upon it, *what* are in this new world the dirigent principles, — the ideal substratum, the ulterior end of all this concernment with the positive interests that so informs that mighty multitude, — he will only be met, as a definite formula, by that same exclusive interest in material triumphs. Orphaned of the profound tradition that attended his birth, the North

American has not yet replaced the inspiring ideality of his past with any high unselfish conception of the future. He lives for the immediate reality of the present, and for this subordinates all his activities in the egoism of material well-being, albeit both individual and collective. Of all his aggregation of the elements of wealth and power, one might say, what Bourget said of the intelligence of his character the Marquis Norbert, "a mountain of wood to which they have not yet known how to set fire." The vital spark is lacking to throw up that flame of the ideal, restless, life-giving, from that mountain of dead wood. Not even the selfishness of patriotism, for want of higher impulses, nor the pride of race, both of which transfigured and exalted in ancient days even the prosaic hardness of the life of Rome, can light a glimmer of ideality or beauty in a people where a cosmopolite confusion and the atomism of a badly understood democracy impede the formation of a veritable national conscience.

One might think that the positivist genius of England has suffered a sea-change in crossing the Atlantic so as to fill its sons there with a spirit deprived of those elements of ideality which tempered it at home, and thus really reducing it to the crudeness which only the exaggeration of passion or satire has ascribed to its English form. For the English spirit, under its rough utilitarian exterior, its mercantile cynicism, its Puritanic severity, always concealed a rare poetic genius and a deep respect for the finer sensibility, which caused Taine to hold that at the bottom of the Teutonic nature, which is the base of the English race, must exist, however modified by the pressure of conquest or the habit of trade, an extraordinary exaltation of the emotional qualities. But the American spirit has not inherited this ancestral poetic instinct, which gushes like

a clear fountain from the British rock
when it is a Moses of high art who touches
it. The English people possess in their in-
stitution of aristocracy (however unequal
and out of date it may appear in the political aspect) a lofty and solid bulwark to
oppose to the shopkeeping spirit and the
encroachment of a prosaic world; so solid
and lofty that Taine could say that since
Grecian times history has presented no example of a society more fit to breed noble
men and a noble spirit. But in the ambient
of America's democracy there are no
heights so lofty as to escape the climbing
of the flood of vulgarity, and it spreads and
extends itself freely as over a level plain.

Sensibility, intelligence, manners —
each is marked in that enormous people
by a radical unaptness for selection; and
this, with the mechanical ordering of their
material activities, makes a chaos of all
that pertains to the realm of the ideal. It
were easy to follow this unaptness from

its most obvious manifestations to the more intimate and essential ones. Prodigal of riches — for meanness is not his fault — the North American has learned only to acquire by them the satisfaction of his vanity and material luxury, but not the chosen note of good taste. In such a surrounding true art can only exist as the rebellion of an individual. Emerson, Poe, are as estrays of a fauna expelled from their true habitat by some geological catastrophe. In "Outre Mer" Bourget speaks of the solemn tone in which the North American utters the word Art, when he, a self-made man, has achieved riches which he now desires to crown with all the human refinements; but he never has felt the divine frenzy of poem or picture; he would buy but to add to his collection a new toy, to satisfy at once his vanity and his acquisitive instinct. That in it which is disinterested, chosen, rare, he ignores, despite the munificence with which he scatters his individual fortune to found schools of art, form popular taste, build splendid museums, patronize huge expositions, and deck his cities with monuments and his streets with bronze and marble. And if one had to characterize his taste, in a word, it would be that which in itself involves the negation of great art; strained brutality of effect, insensibility to soft tones or an exquisite style, the cult of bigness, and that sensationalism which excludes all noble serenity as incompatible with the hurry of his hectic life.

The ideal of beauty does not appeal to the descendants of the austere Puritan, nor even a passionate worship of the truth; they care little for any thinking that has no immediate practical object — it seems to them idle and fruitless; even to science they bring no selfless interest for discovery, nor do they seem capable of loving its truths only because they are true; investigation is merely the necessary antecedent of practical application. Their praiseworthy efforts to extend the benefits of popular education are inspired with the noble motive of communicating the rudiments of knowledge to the masses; but it does not appear that they also concern themselves overmuch with that higher education which shall rise above the general mediocrity. And so the outcome is that of all their struggle with ignorance the only gain has been a sort of universal semiculture and a profound indifference to the higher. . . . As fast as the general ignorance decreases, so, in the air of that giant democracy, decreases the higher learning and vanishes genius itself. This is why the story of their intellectual activity is of a retrogression in brilliance and originality. For while at the era of their Independence and Constitution many famous names illustrate their history in thought as well as in action, a half-century later de Tocqueville could say of them, the Gods are disappearing.

And, when he wrote his master work, there still radiated from Boston, the Puritan home, the city of learning and tradition, a glorious pleiad which holds in the intellectual story of our century a universal fame. Who since has picked up the heritage of Emerson, Channing, Poe? The levelling by the middle classes tends ever, pressing with its desolating task, to plane down what little remains of *intelligentsia:* the flowers are mown by the machine when the weeds remain.

Long since their books have ceased to soar on wings beyond the common vision. To-day the most actual example of what Americans like best in literature must be sought in the gray pages of magazines or periodicals which seldom remind one that that mode of publication was employed in the immortal "Federalist."

In the domain of moral sentiment, the mechanical impulse for the utilitarian has, indeed, encountered a certain balance-wheel in a strong religious tradition; but one may not conclude that even this has given to the direction of conduct a real, disinterested principle. . . . American religiosity, derived from the English and exaggerated, is merely an auxiliary force for the penal law, and would disappear on the day it was found possible without it to give to utilitarian morality that religious sanction which Mill desired for it. The very culmination of that morality is only that of Franklin; a philosophy of conduct which has for its goal a commonplace sagacity, a prudent usefulness, in whose bosom will never rise the emotions of holiness or heroism; and which, fit only to give to one's conscience in the common affairs of life a certain moral support — like the apple-tree cane with which Franklin ever walked — is but a fragile staff with which to surmount great heights. And yet his was its supreme height: it is in the valleys where one must seek for its

actuality. Even if the moral critique were
not to descend below the probity and mod-
eration of Franklin's standard, its necessary termination, as de Tocqueville wisely
said of a society educated narrowly with
similar notions of duty, would surely not be
in that superb and noble decadence which
gives us to measure a Satanic beauty of
tragedy in the downfall of empires, but
rather a kind of pallid materialism, drab
culture, and finally the sleep of an enervation without brilliancy in the silent decay
of all the mainsprings of the moral life. In
that society whose precept tends to put
outside of what is obligatory the higher
manifestations of abnegations and of virtue, practical considerations will always
make the limits of obligation recede indefinitely. And the school of material prosperity, always a rude teacher of repub-
lican austerity, has carried even further
that simplicity of the conception of a rational conduct which now obsesses the

mind. To Franklin's code have succeeded others franker still in their expression of the national wisdom. A book by one Swett Marden was recently [1] published in Boston, "Pushing to the Front," which announced, apparently with much popular approval, as a new moral law, that success is the final end of life; this book was praised even in church circles, and compared to the "Imitation" of à Kempis! . . .

And public life does not escape the consequences of the growth of this germ of disorganization in society generally. Any casual observer of their political customs will tell you how the obsession of material interest tends steadily to enervate and eradicate the sentiment of law or right; the civic virtue of a Hamilton is as an old and rusty sword, every day the more forgotten, lost in the cobwebs of tradition; venality, beginning at the polls, spreads through the working of all their institu-

[1] 1894. The book seems to have had less effect than Rodó feared.

tions; the government by a mediocrity
renders vain that emulation which exalts
the character and the intelligence, and im-
poses itself even on the imagination as an
unavoidable future. A democracy not subject to a superior instruction, not trained
in liberal schools to the understanding of
true human excellence, tends always to
that abominable brutality of the majority
which despises the greater moral benefits
of liberty and annuls in public opinion all
respect for the dignity of the individual.
And to-day a new and formidable power
arises to accentuate this absolutism of
numbers: the political influence of a plu-
tocracy represented only by the agents of
the trusts, monopolies of production, and
lords of the economic life, one of the most
noteworthy and significant features of the
United States of to-day. Their advent has
caused almost everybody to recall to mind
the coming of that proud and over-rich
class which at the end of the Roman Re-

public preceded the tyranny of the Cæsars
and the ruin of liberty. And the exclusive
preoccupation with material aggrandizement, the deity of such a civilization, has
its logical result on the State as on the individual, putting the *struggle-for-life* principle also at the head of national policy,
and making its representative the supreme
personification of the national energy —
the *postulant* of Emerson, the ruling *per-
sonage* of Taine.

To the impulse which drives the spiritual life toward that deorientation of the
ideal to the selfishly useful corresponds
physically that other principle which in
the astounding increase of that people im-
pels both the multitude and the initiative
ever in the direction of that boundless
West which in the times of their first independence was all mystery, veiled behind
the forests of the Mississippi. In fact that
improvised West — which grows so formidable to the older Atlantic States and

already claims hegemony in the near future — is where the most faithful represen-
tation of American life is to be found at
this moment of its evolution. It is there
where the definite results, the logical and
natural fruits of the spirit that has guided
the great democracy from its origin, are
brought into relief for the observer so that
he can picture to himself the aspect of its
immediate future. To the Virginian, the
Yankee, has succeeded the master of the
yesterday empty prairies, of whom Michel
Chevalier predicted, half a century since,
"The last shall one day be the first."
Utilitarianism, empty of all ideal content,
a certain cosmopolitan levity of spirit, and
the levelling of a falsely conceived democracy, will in him reach their ultimate victory. Every noble element of that civilization, all which binds it to the generous
traditions and lofty origin of its historic
dignity — the arrival of the men of the
Mayflower, the memory of the Patricians

of Virginia and the warriors of New England, the spirit of the people and lawmakers of the Emancipation — will remain only in the older States, where a Boston or a Philadelphia still maintain "the palladium of the Washingtonian tradition." Chicago will arise to reign. And its overweening superiority over the original States of the Atlantic shore is based on its belief that they are reactionary, too European, too subject to tradition. History confers no claims on any, where popular election confers the purple.

As fast as the utilitarian genius of that nation takes on a more defined character, franker, narrower yet, with the intoxication of material prosperity, so increases the impatience of its sons to spread it abroad by propaganda, and think it predestined for all humanity. To-day they openly aspire to the primacy of the world's civilization, the direction of its ideas, and think themselves the forerunners of all culture that is to prevail. The colloquial phrase, ironically quoted by Laboulaye, "America can beat the world," is taken seriously by almost any virile Westerner. At the bottom of their open rivalry with Europe lies a contempt for it that is almost naïve, and the profound conviction that within a brief period they are destined to eclipse its glory and do away with its spiritual superiority; thus once more fulfilling, in the progress of civilization, the hard law of the ancient mysteries, whereby the initiated shall put to death the initiator. It were useless to seek to convince them that, although their services to inventions and material advance have been doubtless great, even rising to the measure of a universal human obligation, they do not of themselves suffice to alter the axis of the earth. It were useless to seek to convince them that the fires lit upon European altars, the work done by peoples living these three thousand years gone by about the shores of the Medi-

terranean, though rising to glorious genius
when bound with the olive and the palm of
Athens, a work still being carried on and
in whose traditions and teachings we
South Americans live, makes a sum which
cannot be equalled by any equation of
Washington plus Edison. Would they
even revise the Book of Genesis, to put
themselves upon the front page?

But, aside from the insufficiency of the
part that is given them to play in the education of humanity, their own character
itself precludes all possibility of their hegemony. Nature has not granted them
the genius for propaganda, the vocation of
the apostle. They lack that great gift of
amiability — likeableness, in a lofty sense;
that extraordinary power of sympathy
with which those races endowed by Provi-
dence for the task of education know how
to make of their culture a beauty, as did
Greece, loveable, eternal, and yet always
with something of their own.

North American civilization may abound
— it does abound — in fertile suggestions,
profitable examples; it may inspire admiration, astonishment, respect; but it is rare
for the foreigner to feel his heart come to
his mouth with strong emotion when first
he sees that Bartholdi statue holding high
its torch of Liberty over New York Har-
bour; that thrill profound with which the
ancient traveller saw the rosy light of the
marble and the sheen of Athena's spear
over the early dawn on the Acropolis.

But please remember that when I, in
the name of their soul's rights, deny to
their utilitarianism the right to impose itself as typical of the future on the world
as mould or model, I do not in the least as-
sert that its labours are wasted even in relation to those things which we may call
soul-interests. . . . Without the arm which
clears and constructs, there might now
be no shelter for the brain that thinks;
without some certain conquest of the

materialities, the rule of the spiritualities in human societies becomes impossible. Renan's aristocratic idealism recognized, even from the point of view of the moral interest of the race and its future spiritual development, the import of the utilitarian labour of this century; "To get away from need is to redeem oneself." In the remote past even the prosaic and selfish activities of the merchant resulted in putting for the first time a people in relation with others, and thus had a far-reaching effect on men's ideas; since this had much to do with multiplying the means of intelligence, refining and softening manners, perhaps even showing the way to a more advanced morality; and the same positive force appears later, favouring the higher ideals of civilization. It was the gold accumulated by the merchants of the Italian republics that paid, says Saint-Victor, for the works of the Renaissance. The ships that came back from the countries of the

Thousand and One Nights, laden with ivory and spices, made it possible for Lorenzo di Medici to renew in Florentine merchants' houses the feast of Plato. All history shows a definite relation of growth between the progress of utilitarian activity and the ideal. And just as the former can be turned into a shelter and protection for the latter, so the ideas of the mind often give rise to utilitarian results, above all when these latter are not sought directly. For instance, Bagehot remarks that the immense positive benefits of navigation might never have been attained for humanity if in earliest times there had not been dreamers, apparently idle — and certainly misunderstood by their contemporaries — who were interested solely in the contemplation of the movements of the stars.

This law of harmony bids us also respect the arm that labours arduously in what seems a barren and prosaic soil. The work of North American positivism will also at the end serve the cause of Ariel. That which this people of Cyclops have achieved for the direct purpose of material advantage, with all their sense for what is useful and their admirable faculty of mechanical invention, will be converted by other peoples, or later, even by themselves, to a wealth of material for the higher selection. Thus that most precious and fundamental invention of the alphabet, which gives the wings of immortality to the spoken word, originated in Phœnician shops, the discovery of merchants who only desired to keep their accounts. Using it for purposes merely mercenary, they never dreamed that the genius of a superior race would transfigure and transform it to a means of perpetuating the light and the learning of their own being. The relation between material good and good that is intellectual or moral is thus only a new aspect of that modern doctrine which we call the transformation of energy; material well-being may be transformed into spiritual superiority.

But North American life does not as yet offer us any new example of this indiscutable relation, nor even dimly suggest it as the triumph of the generation to come.

Our wish and our belief, indeed, incline us to hope that a superior destiny may be reserved for that civilization in a time not too remote for prophecy; the more that, under the spur of their energy, even the brief time that separates them from their dawn has sufficed to satisfy the expenditure of the vitality required for such immense achievement. Their past, their present, must be but the entry-way to a great future. Yet all shows that this is still far away from its definitive. The assimilative energy which has so far enabled them to maintain a certain uniformity as well as some touch of genius, despite the enormous inrush of ethnic elements opposed to

those which have so far made the basis of
their character, will have to do battle every
day more strenuous, and in their utilitarianism, which proscribes all ideality, will
find no inspiration sufficiently strong to
maintain their solidarity with the older
ideal. The illustrious thinker, who compared the slave of olden times to an atom
outside the attraction of the social orbit,
might well use the same comparison to
characterize that numerous colony of German origin now peopling the Middle and
Northern West, which preserves intact in
their nature, their society, and their customs, the impression of that German spirit
which in many of its profoundest and
strongest characteristics must be considered as the actual antithesis of the American. . . . And also, a civilization which is
destined to survive and spread throughout
the world; which has not mummified itself in the manner of the Chinese by losing
all capability of change; cannot indefi-

nitely prolong the direction of its energies to one order of things alone. Let us hope, then, that the spirit of that Titanic organism, which has so far been utility and will-power only, may some day also be intelligence, sentiment, ideality; that from that mighty forge may arise, in last result, the noble human figure, harmonious, select, that Spencer foreshadowed in the discourse I have adverted to. But we may not look for him in the present reality of that people, nor in their immediate future; and we must give up hoping to find the perfect type of an exemplary civilization in what is now but a rough sketch, huge and misshapen, having to pass through many correcting hands before it assumes the serene, the perfect shape of a people that have fully developed their genius and contemplate their work, *finis coronat*, gloriously crowned. So, in his "Dream of the Condor," Leconte de Lisle depicts the ascension on strong wings and at last the Olympian tranquillity far above the snowpeaks of the Cordilleras!

Before posterity, before history, every great people ought to appear as a growth whose harmonious development has produced a fruit whose fine essence offers to the future the fragrance of its ideality and a fecund seed. Without this durable, human result, raised above the transitory end of the immediately useful, the power and grandeur of empires are but as dreams of a night in the existence of man, to be unheeded, uncounted in the doings of the day which weave the world's destiny. A great civilization, a great people, in the eye of history, is that which after its time has passed still leaves the chords of its memory vibrating, its spirit a lasting legacy to posterity, a new and divine portion of the sum of things. So Carlyle said of the souls of his heroes. So when Helena, in Goethe's poem, called from the realms of night, returns again to the shades, she leaves to

Faust her tunic and her veil; the vestments
are not herself, but as she has worn them,
they breathe of her divineness and possess
ever a spell to elevate the soul of him who
keeps them above all vulgar things.

An organized society which limits its
idea of civilization to the accumulation of
material abundance, and of justice to their
equitable distribution among its members,
will never make of its great cities anything
that differs essentially from the heaping-up
of anthills. Populous, opulent cities do not
suffice to make a civilization immutable,
intensive; they are, indeed, necessary for
the highest culture, are its natural atmosphere; the soul of the great man can
rarely grow from amid the petty interests
of small towns; but this quantitative side
of a nation's greatness, like the size of its
armies, is but means, not results. Of the
stones of Carthage not one remains to bear
any message of light, and all the immen-
sity of Babylon or Nineveh does not fill in

human memory the hollow of man's hand as compared with the few furlongs that lie between the Acropolis and the Piræus. In the perspective of the ideal no city appears great, though it occupy all the space around the towers of Nimrod, nor strong because it can build again those Babylonian walls which carried six chariots abreast; nor beautiful because it was paved with flagstones of alabaster and girt with the gardens of Semiramis. . . . No. In this view that city only is great whose spirit's barriers extend far beyond the mountains or the seas, whose very name pronounced illuminates for posterity an epoch of human thought, a horizon of history. It is strong and lovely when its days are something more than the invariable repetition of the same echo, repeated in never-ending circle; when in it there is something which floats above the faces of the crowd; when amid its night lights there are the lamps which light the solitude of vigils devoted

only to thought; thoughts whence germi-
nate ideas which are to come to the sunlight of the coming day with a cry to
humanity, a force that shall compel men's
souls.

Then only may the extent and material
greatness of the city measure the intensity
of its civilization. Royal capitals, avenues
of proud palaces, are a narrower home
than the desert for man's thinking when
it is not thought that overlords them. In
Tennyson's "Maud" there is a symbol
of this torturing of the soul when man's
society leaves it still in solitude; where the
hero in his madness dreams himself to
be dead and buried but a few feet under-
ground, beneath a London pavement; and
his consciousness remains, despite his
death, attached to the poor remains of his
body; the confused clamour of the street
makes a dull rumbling that shakes his narrow tomb and impedes his every dream of
peace; the weight of an indifferent multi-

tude weighs heavily above his grave, the heavy tread of horses seems to trample on it with disdain; the days succeed days with inexorable tedium. And Maud would wish her grave still farther, farther down, deeper yet within the earth; the dim noises of its surface serve but to keep alive the consciousness that she is dead.

Already there exist, in our Latin America, cities whose material grandeur and apparent civilization place them in the first rank; but one may fear lest a touch of thought upon their exterior, so sumptuous, may make the shining vessel ring hollow within; lest our cities too — though they had their Moreno, their Rivadavia, their Sarmiento, cities which gave initiative to an immortal revolution that, like a stone cast on water, spread the glory of their heroes and the words of their tribunes in ever-widening circles over a vast continent — may end like Tyre or Sidon, or as Carthage ended.

It is your generation that must prevent this; the youth which is of to-day, blood and muscle and nerve of the future. I speak to you, seeing in you those who are destined to guide the others in coming battles for a spiritual cause. The perseverance of your strength must be in you as your certainty of victory. Be not afraid to preach the evangel of refinement to the Scythians, of intelligence to the Bœotians, of disinterest to the Phœnicians. It is enough that thought insists on being, on showing that it exists, as Diogenes proved of movement, to make its spread irresistible and its ultimate triumph secure. Palm by palm, of its own impulse, it will win what space it needs to establish its kingdom among all the other manifestations of life. In its physical organization it will elevate and augment the hollow of the very skull it works in, by its own activity: the thinking races in their physiological growth reveal this power of the

unseen workman within. In his social organization also will the thinker well know
how to broaden the stage for his drama
without the intervention of any power alien
to his own. But that conviction, which
should preserve from a discouragement
whose one utility is to make us rid ourselves of the mean and mediocre, should
also keep us from the impatience which
demands from time any alteration of its
majestic rhythm.

Every one who devotes himself to prop-
agate and preserve in contemporary America a disinterested ideal of the soul — art,
science, ethics, religious belief, a political
policy of ideals — should educate his belief
in the persevering preparation for the future. The past belonged entirely to the
sword arm; the present seems well-nigh
given over to the horny hand that clears
away and builds; the future — a future that
seems all the nearer as the thinking and
willing of those who look forward to it

grow more earnest — shall offer the sta-
bility, the scenario, the right atmosphere,
to make possible the higher evolution of
man's soul.

Can you not picture to yourselves the
America we others dream of? Hospitable
to things of the spirit, and not only to the
immigrant throngs; thoughtful, without
sacrificing its energy of action; serene and
strong and withal full of generous enthusiasm; resplendent with the charm of
morning calm like the smile of a waking
infant, yet with the light of awakening
thought. Think on her at least; the honour of your future history depends on your
keeping constantly before your eyes the
vision of that America, radiant above the
realities of the present like the rose window
above the dark nave of a cathedral. . . .
You may not be its founders; but you will at
all events be its forerunners. In the glories
of the future there be also palms for such.
To prepare the advent of a new human

type, a new social unity, a profound student of history, Edgar Quinet, has observed that there always precedes, long before, a scattered group, premature, whose rôle in the evolution of society is like that of the prophetic species in biology discovered by Héer. The new type begins by barely signalizing individualities; these later get organized into varieties, and finally these last, encountering a favouring medium, attain the rank of a species; then, says Quinet, the "group" becomes the multitude, and rules.

This is why your moral philosophy, in labour or in combat, should be the reverse of the Horatian *carpe diem;* treat the present moment only as the first step in the stairway you are to tread, or as a breach in the enemy wall you are to enter by. Ask not at once for the final victory, but for bettering your conditions for the conflict. Thus will your energy have the greater stimulus, since the dramatic interest is greater in the continual renewal and advance, fit school to purify the forces of an heroic generation, than in the serene and Olympic attitude in which a golden age might invest the acolytes of its glory. "It is not the possession of good things, but their attainment which gives to man delight and glory in his power," said Taine, speaking of the happy times of the Renaissance.

Perhaps it were an audacious and ingenuous hope to believe in so rapid and fortunate an evolution, so efficacious an employment of your powers, as to expect that the span of your own generation will suffice to bring in America the conditions of intellectual life; from our now primitive surroundings a true social interest; from our present dead level a summit which shall really be supreme. But where there may not be entire transformation there may be progress; and even though you know that the first fruits of the soil you labour may not be yours, they will if you

are generous and brave be a new stimulus
to action. The best work is that which is
realized without impatience for immediate
success, the most glorious effort that which
places the goal beyond the visible horizon,
and the purest abnegation that which re-
nounces for the present, not indeed the
laurel of men's applause, but the bliss of
seeing one's labour consummate and its
goal attained.

Antiquity had altars "for the unknown
Gods." Consecrate a part of your soul to
the unknown future. As societies develop,
thought for the future becomes more and
more a factor in their growth and an
inspiration to their labours. From the
blind improvidence of the savage, who
only sees in it that time which shall bring
him to the setting of the day's sun and
conceives not how his lot in other days
may be determined by his present action,
up to our anxious preoccupation with the
future and provision for our posterity,

there is an immense distance; yet even this may seem little enough some day. We are only capable of progress in so far as we can adapt our actions every day to the conditions of a more distant future, to countries farther and farther away. Assurance of our part in bringing about a work which shall survive us, fruitful in times to come, exalts our human dignity and gives us triumph even over the limitations of our nature. If unhappily humanity had to despair definitely of the immortality of the individual consciousness, the most religious sentiment that it could substitute would be that which comes of the thought that even after our dissolution into the heart of things there would outlast, as part of all human inheritance, the very best of all that we had felt or thought, our deepest and our purest essence — just as the beams of a long-extinguished star go on indefinitely and still cheer us mortals, albeit with a melancholy light.

The future is, in the life of human societies, the one inspiring thought. From
pious veneration of the past and the cult
of tradition, on the one hand, and, on the
other, a daring impulse toward the future,
comes the noble force which, uplifting the
common thought above the present limitations, imparts to its collective agitations
and sentiments a sense for some ideal.
Men and peoples work under the inspiration of ideas, as the beasts by instinct; and
that society which labours and struggles,
even unconsciously, to impose an idea
upon actualities, acts as does the bird
who, building its nest at the prompting of
some inner imagination, obeys at once an
unconscious memory of the past and a
mysterious presentiment of the future.

A preoccupation for the ulterior destiny
of our life, by eliminating any suggestion
of self-interest, purifies and tranquillizes
it and also ennobles; and it is a proud
honour of this century that the impelling

force of this thought for the future, this sense of what is due the dignity of a rational being, should have shown itself so clearly. Even in the depths of the most utter pessimism, in the bosom of that bitter metaphysic which brought from the East the love of dissolution and nonentity, even Hartmann, the apostle for the return to the Unconscious, has preached, and with some appearance of logic, the austere duty of going on with the work of improvement, labouring for the good of the future, so that human effort, aiding evolution, may bring about a more rapid impulse to the final end — which is the termination of all sorrow, and likewise of all life.

But not, as did Hartmann, in the name of death, but in that of life and hope do I ask of you a portion of your soul for the labour for the future ; and it is to ask this of you that I have sought inspiration in the gentle and lovely image of my Ariel. The bounti-

ful Spirit whom Shakespeare hit upon to
clothe with so high a symbolism, perhaps
with that divine unconsciousness of all it
meant which is common to great geniuses,
shows clearly, even in this statuette, its
ideal significance, admirably expressed in
the sculptor's lines. Ariel is reason, and
the higher truth. Ariel is that sublime sentiment of the perfectibility of man through
whose virtue human clay is magnified and
transformed in the realm of things for each
one who lives by his light — even that miserable clay of which Ahriman spoke to
Manfred. . . . Ariel is, to nature, that
crowning of its work which ends the as-
cending process of organic life with the call
of the spirit. Ariel triumphant signifies
ideality and order in life, noble inspiration
in thought, unselfishness in conduct, high
taste in art, heroism of action, delicacy and
refinement in manners and usages. He is
the eponymous hero in the épopée of man,
the immortal protagonist, since first his

presence inspired the feeble struggles of reason in primitive man, when he first knitted his brow in the effort to shape the flint, or to scratch rude drawings on a reindeer's bones; since first with his arms he fanned the sacred fire which the ancient Aryan, progenitor of the peoples we call civilized, lit, by what mystery we know not, on the banks of the Ganges, and forged from the divine flame the sceptre of man's mastery. Ariel accompanies him still, and onward, breeding races ever higher, until at the end he hovers radiant above those souls which have over-passed the natural limit of humanity; the same for Plato on the Sunium Promontory as for Francis of Assisi on the solitude of the Albern Mont. His invincible power has as its impulse every uplifting moment of a human life. Though overcome a thousand and one times by the untamable rebellion of Caliban, proscribed by the victorious barbarian, smothered in the clouds of battle, his bright wings spotted by trailing in "the eternal dunghill of Job," Ariel ever rises again, immortally renews his beauty and his youth. Ariel runs nimbly as at the call of Prospero to all who really care for him and seek to find him. His kindly power goes even out at times to those who would deny him. He guides the blind forces of evil and ignorance often to aid, and unwittingly, in works of good. He crosses human history with a song, as in the "Tempest," to inspire those who labour and those who fight until he brings about the fulfilment of that divine plan to them unknown — and he is permitted, as in Shakespeare's play, to snap his bonds in twain and soar forever into his circle of diviner light.

And more than for these words of mine I would have you ever remember tenderly this little figure of Ariel. I would that the image, light and graceful, of this bronze, impress itself upon your inmost spirit. . . . Once I saw, in a museum, an old coin;

worn and effaced I could still read its device, in the thin gold, the one word *Espe-
ranza*. I pondered on the influence that
simple inscription might have had on the
many generations through whose hands
the coin had passed ; how many fainting
spirits it had cheered, how many generous
impulses it had fostered, how many des-
perate resolutions it had prevented. So
may the figure of this bronze, graven in
your hearts, fulfil in your lives this invisible yet determining part. In dark hours
of discouragement may it rekindle in your
conscience the warmth of the ideal, return
to your hearts the glow of a perishing hope.
And Ariel, first enthroned behind the bas-
tion of your inner life, may sally thence to
the attack and conquering of other souls.
I see the bright spirit smiling back upon
you in future times, even though your own
still works in shadow. I have faith in your
will and in your strength, even more in
those to whom you shall transfer your life,

transmit your work. I dream in rapture of that day when realities shall convince the world that the Cordillera which soars above the continent of the Americas has been carved to be the pedestal of this statue, the altar of the cult of Ariel.

So spoke Prospero. The youths departed, after a filial grasping of the Master's hand. Of his sweet words there lingered an echo in each one's mind as when a finger is drawn across a musical glass. It was the last hour of eve. A ray of the dying sun fell through the shadowed hall, and touching the front of bronze seemed almost to animate the face of the figure with the unquiet spark of life; and the ray prolonged itself as if the genius imprisoned in the bronze were sending his last look toward the young men going away. . . . For a long time they walked in silence. Guarded by their common absorption each soul could feel that fine distilling of medi-

tation that falls on thought like quiet dew
on the wool of sleeping lambs. When the
rough contact of the street crowds roused
them, it was already night; a serene, soft
night of summer. The grace and calm that
dropped from its ebon urn over the land
rose above the prosy realities of the things
of men; only their presence brought the
youths again back to earth. A soft breeze
charged the air with a languid, delicious
sense of abandon, like the trembling of the
cup in a Bacchante's hand. The darkness
in the heavens was not of black, but rather
of a deep azure that seemed expressive of a
thoughtful calm. Enamelled in it the great
stars blazed amid their infinite company:
Aldebaran, arrayed in purple light; Sirius,
like the hollow of a silver chalice turned
toward the world; the Cross, whose arms
are open over our America as if to guard
and hold its final hope. . . .

And then it was that after a prolonged
silence the youngest of the group — they

called him ''Enjolrás'' because of his ardent thought — spoke, pointing out first the idle movement of the human herd and then the radiant beauty of the skies:

''See . . . while the crowd goes by, it never looks up to the heavens: yet they look down upon the multitude . . . something descends upon the indifferent mass . . . the vibration of the stars reminds me of the waving arms of a sower, sowing seed. . . .''

THE END